DATE DUE			

E. L. Doctorow

Twayne's United States Authors Series

Warren French, Editor

University of Wales, Swansea

TUSAS 562

E. L. Doctorow
Photograph reproduced by permission of Barbara Walz.

E. L. Doctorow

By Carol C. Harter
and James R. Thompson

Ohio University

Twayne Publishers
A Division of G. K. Hall & Co. • *Boston*

E. L. Doctorow
Carol C. Harter and James R. Thompson

Copyright 1990 by G. K. Hall & Co.
All rights reserved.
Published by Twayne Publishers
A division of G. K. Hall & Co.
70 Lincoln Street
Boston, Massachusetts 02111

Copyediting supervised by Barbara Sutton.
Book production by Janet Z. Reynolds.
Book design by Barbara Anderson.
Typeset in 11 pt. Garamond by Compositors Corp., Cedar Rapids, Iowa.

First published 1990.
10 9 8 7 6 5 4 3 2 1

Library of Congress Cataloging-in-Publication Data

Harter, Carol C.
    E. L. Doctorow / by Carol C. Harter and James R. Thompson.
        p.   cm. — (Twayne's United States authors series ; TUSAS 562)
    Includes bibliographical references.
    ISBN 0-8057-7604-4 (alk. paper)
    1. Doctorow, E. L., 1931–   —Criticism and interpretation.
    I. Thompson, James R.   II. Title.   III. Series.
PS3554.03Z69   1990
813′.54—dc20   89-24630
                                                            CIP

For Michael, Sean, Tracey and Javan

Contents

About the Authors
Preface
Acknowledgments
Chronology

Chapter One
The Life and Art of E. L. Doctorow: "The Passion of
Our Calling" 1

Chapter Two
"A Relentlessly Revisionist Spirit": *Welcome to Hard
Times* and *Big as Life* 13

Chapter Three
"The Contingency of Song": *The Book of Daniel* 26

Chapter Four
Ragtime and the Vision of Circularity: "The World
Composed and Recomposed" 49

Chapter Five
Loon Lake and the Vision of Synchronicity: "Exactly
Like You" 72

Chapter Six
"A Mind Looking for Its Own Geography":
Drinks before Dinner, Lives of the Poets, and
World's Fair 95

Afterword: Doctorow at Fifty-five 120
Notes and References 123
Selected Bibliography 133
Index 137

About the Authors

Carol C. Harter is currently president and professor of English at the State University of New York College of Arts and Science at Geneseo. She formerly served as associate professor and held several administrative posts at Ohio University, Athens. She received a B.A. with honors from Harpur College and an M.A. and Ph.D. from the State University of New York at Binghamton with a "distinguished" dissertation on Faulkner. In addition to performing administrative duties and writing about management issues, Harter continues to teach and write on American literary topics. She has published articles on various American writers, including Emerson, Dreiser, Eliot, Faulkner, Joyce Carol Oates, and several Ohio-based writers, and is particularly interested in contemporary American novelists.

James R. Thompson is professor of English and American literature at Ohio University, Athens. He received B.A. and M.A. degrees from Bowling Green State University and a Ph.D. from the University of Cincinnati, where he was a Howard Taft Fellow. Thompson has written and lectured on the English romantic poets and on American fiction, and he was a Fulbright lecturer on American literature at the University of Graz, Austria. He has previously authored *Leigh Hunt* and *Thomas Lovell Beddoes* in Twayne's English Authors Series.

Harter and Thompson coauthored *John Irving* for Twayne's United States Authors Series, in 1986, and at present are collaborating on a study of the uses of history in contemporary American fiction.

Preface

In addition to a collection of short fiction and an experimental play, E. L. Doctorow has published six novels since 1960, at least three of which have earned him extensive critical respect and one—his 1975 *Ragtime*—enormous popularity. To be both widely read and respectable remains a rare achievement, especially because, as in Doctorow's case, each additional work bravely charts new technical and stylistic territory rather than exploits previous successes. At this time only one of his books is out of print, and this is because of his own dissatisfaction with it.

Admonishing a questioner who had imputed to his fiction a particular nexus of ethnicity and sexual emphasis, E. L. Doctorow remarked, "You here have a particular responsibility to distinguish literary criticism from demonology." The great richness and variety of his work has, however, already generated a sizeable and heterogeneous body of criticism—one book and two collections of essays—some of which, we suspect, he might well consider demonology.[1] Our own goal has been to provide a comprehensive introduction to the entire range of his fiction and also, while attempting to add our own contributions to the understanding of his work, to suggest (both in the text and bibliography) the nature and direction of some of that accumulated scholarship. We hope that in so doing this examination of Doctorow's novels avoids the demonological; we have tried to steer clear of critical excesses of all kinds, preferring to risk understating both aesthetic and thematic arguments rather than to distort the work. In what follows, however, our preference has generally been for literary analysis rather than ideological commentary; the latter has already preoccupied many of the novelist's admirers and detractors and not infrequently distorted his excellent fiction.

After an introduction to the writer and his work, subsequent chapters deal with his fiction as it emerged chronologically. Our focus is on the integrity and significance of individual works, but we also attempt such synthesis as is possible for a writer whose technical and thematic range is great.

Carol C. Harter

Ohio University

James R. Thompson

Ohio University

Acknowledgments

We are grateful to Random House for permission to quote from *Drinks Before Dinner, Lives of the Poets* and *World's Fair*, and to Barbara Walz for permission to use her fine photograph of the author.

We wish to once again thank Roseann Sedwick for her cheerful patience and superb secretarial skills. We also wish to acknowledge the enormous generosity and editorial direction of Warren French who has, once again, provided essential guidance.

Chronology

1931   Edgar Lawrence Doctorow born 6 January to David and Rose Doctorow in the Bronx, New York.

1948   Graduates from Bronx High School of Science.

1948–1952   Attends Kenyon College; studies under John Crowe Ransom.

1952   Receives A.B. in philosophy, Kenyon College.

1952–1953   Does graduate work in literature and drama, Columbia University.

1953–1955   Drafted into the army; serves in Germany.

1954   Marries Helen Setzer, whose pen name is now Henslee.

1959–1964   Senior editor at New American Library.

1960   *Welcome to Hard Times.*

1964–1969   Editor in chief at Dial Press.

1966   *Big as Life.*

1968–1969   Vice president at Dial Press.

1969–1970   Writer in residence, University of California at Irvine, the first of a number of such positions he has held, including posts at Sarah Lawrence, Princeton, the Yale School of Drama, and New York University.

1971   *The Book of Daniel*; Guggenheim Fellowship.

1975   *Ragtime.*

1976   Wins National Book Critics Circle Award for *Ragtime*.

1978   "Drinks before Dinner" produced by Joseph Papp.

1979   *Drinks before Dinner.*

1980   *Loon Lake.*

1984   *Lives of the Poets.*

1985   *World's Fair.*

1986   Receives American Book Award for *World's Fair*.

1989   *Billy Bathgate.*

Chapter One

The Life and Art of
E. L. Doctorow:
"The Passion of Our Calling"

Perhaps fewer than a handful of novelists on the contemporary American scene possess the breadth of thematic interests, the technical virtuosity, and the simultaneous appeal to serious and popular audiences alike that E. L. Doctorow displays. Moreover, there are fewer still whose literary oeuvre to date is so rich and so strikingly varied. No two books by Doctorow resemble each other in any overt way; while the insistent obsession with the American past may be said to be the thread that connects his major works to one another, the manifestations of that obsession are remarkably distinct and original. As Peter Prescott has noted, each new book offers a surprise: "The distinguishing characteristic of E. L. Doctorow's work is its double vision. In each of his books he experiments with forms of fiction . . . in each, he develops a tone, a structure and a texture that he hasn't used before. At the same time, he's a deeply traditional writer, reworking American history, American literary archetypes, even exhausted subliterary genres. It's an astonishing performance, really."[1]

And astonishing it is. Doctorow's fictional range has continued to widen from the publication in 1960 of his first novel, *Welcome to Hard Times,* a terse, acerbic, and powerful fable in the form of an antiwestern, to the publication in 1985 of the finely textured and evocative autobiographical novel, *World's Fair*—thus reversing the usual tendency of writers to open their careers with fiction based on their own lives. In between came the science fiction novel *Big as Life* in 1966 (the only book Doctorow regrets and hence the only one currently out of print), in 1972 his intensely charged *The Book of Daniel,* in 1975 the innovative and widely acclaimed *Ragtime,* and in 1980 the very ambitious *Loon Lake.* In addition to a small but influential group of essays and an experimental play, *Drinks before Dinner,* 1979, Doctorow has also published *Lives of the Poets* in 1984, a collection of stories and a novella with an overarching novelistic unity.[2]

"A Writer's Life"

"The minute you ask a question about a writer's life, you're not dealing with the book," Doctorow has said; moreover he claims that nothing in his own life—that is in his external existence—really matters: "My life is very quiet, dull bourgeois. A wife and three terrific children. We have a close family life. Sometimes I teach. I tend not to get in fights in bars. I don't go hunting for big game in Africa. I don't box. I love tennis."[3] Yet if E. L. Doctorow has lived a quiet (though intellectually and creatively vigorous) life, he was nonetheless able to write a 288-page book—*World's Fair*—based on the first nine years of his childhood. That novel finds significance in the fabric of a boy's everyday life in the New York City of the 1930s; it demonstrates that the fiction writer need not have experienced the turbulent and romantic life of a Hemingway, to which Doctorow ironically alludes—shot big game in Africa or roughhoused in bars—in order to write important novels.

Edgar Lawrence Doctorow was born in New York City on 6 January 1931, to David and Rose Doctorow, children of Russian Jewish immigrants. Both the immigrant status—"the immigrated universe" (*Lives,* 94)—and the Jewish culture with which he often equates it were major influences on his life. Doctorow was bar mitzvahed and received traditional Jewish training; Jewish cultural inheritance has everywhere marked his fiction (but most clearly in *The Book of Daniel*), from specific ethnic details to general outlook. But his free-thinking grandfather and his father established the affective intellectual milieu: "I grew up in a lower-middle class environment of generally enlightened, socialist sensibility. My grandfather was a printer, an intellectual, a chess player, atheist, and a socialist." It was, he tells us, "a very Jewish thing, somehow."[4] What he describes here is a particular configuration of ethnicity and political views that has produced many brilliant New York intellectuals and artists; but its legacy for Doctorow was secular and eclectic, setting him apart from a more general Jewish heritage and freeing him for the far-ranging speculation that would become the hallmark of his fiction. His father was "a romantic, a dreamer" (*EC,* 53), who owned and lost a record, radio, and musical instrument store and then became a salesman.

After graduating from the prestigious Bronx High School of Science, Doctorow attended an equally fine institution, Kenyon College in Ohio, studying philosophy under several notable scholars and literature under John Crowe Ransom; poet James Wright was a classmate and friend. After receiving his A.B. in philosophy in 1952, he undertook graduate study at Columbia University. Drafted into the Army in 1953, he served part of the next two years in Germany; during his tour of duty he married Helen Setzer, whom he had met while at Columbia. Doctorow spent the lean years following military service doing various odd jobs, including spending periods of time as a reader for both CBS Television and Columbia Pictures. In 1959 he joined New American Library, where he became senior editor; when he resigned from that post in 1964 it was to assume the role of editor in chief at Dial Press, where he became vice president in 1968. While at Dial, Doctorow published his first novel, *Welcome to Hard Times* (1960); he had had, by that time, a considerable amount of experience with popular fiction and films and had come to believe that he could "lie better" (*EC,* 34) than did the writers he had read professionally.

In 1969 he left publishing for good, taking a teaching job in creative writing at the University of California at Irvine (1969–70). This was the first of a number of such teaching positions he has held over the years, including posts at Sarah Lawrence, Princeton, the Yale School of Drama, and New York University, where he currently teaches. There is, however, little of the academic writer about Doctorow—he has perhaps spent too many years in professional publishing—and he has in fact indicated little enthusiasm for the proliferation of university writing programs in recent years.

In 1971, two years after leaving Dial Press, Doctorow published his third novel, *The Book of Daniel.* His second book, *Big as Life,* had come out five years earlier but had satisfied neither himself, his publisher, nor the reading public. *Daniel,* however, was much more successful in every way and, settling in to the writer's life, Doctorow would produce his subsequent novels at regular intervals: *Ragtime* (1975), *Loon Lake* (1980), *World's Fair* (1985). In 1978 his experimental play, *Drinks before Dinner,* was performed and, in the following year, published. *Lives of the Poets,* a collection of short fiction, was published in 1984.

Ragtime won the National Book Critics Award for fiction and *World's Fair* received the American Book Award. Films have been made of *Hard Times, Daniel* and *Ragtime,* in the case of the latter, quite successfully. The last three novels, especially the enormously popular *Ragtime,* have made him what he is now—a very affluent and critically admired urban writer, with an old home in New Rochelle (the setting and partial inspiration for *Ragtime*), a house at Sag Harbor (where he wrote *World's Fair*), and, like the protagonist of *Lives,* an apartment near New York University for his periods of teaching. In this regard, he may be contrasted with John Cheever and John Updike, both of whom live in the suburban ethos and embody it in their fiction.

Doctorow, affable, reserved, looking distinguished in black tie, can be found helping the Book-of-the-Month Club—that most establishment of institutions—celebrate its sixtieth anniversary of spreading literary culture through the American middle class. But the same writer is just as much at home at the forty-eighth annual congress of International PEN, scolding an embattled Norman Mailer for having invited President Reagan's Secretary of State, George Shultz, to give the opening address. Interviews reveal a deeply thoughtful, skeptical, often humorous man, acutely aware of the innumerable problems of authorship in the late twentieth century, but still intensely committed to its humanistic potential.

The Writer as Adversary

Doctorow, as numerous critics and the writer himself have noted, is a rare phenomenon in American letters, a white male novelist whose concerns clearly embrace and engage the larger social and political issues of our past and our present. While for Günter Grass, Nadine Gordimer, Milan Kundera, Alexander Solzhenitsyn or Tadeusz Konwicki such involvement would be taken for granted, American writers from Emerson and Thoreau to the present often define their roles in terms of the drama of the private self, a legacy, perhaps, of the Puritan obsession with the separate soul. Doctorow's own view is that "solitude, profound solitude as much as society, has been an overriding condition in American literary history."[5] He believes that the failure of American writers to commit themselves to public issues, especially after the failure of such involvement in the 1930s, has produced novelists who "tend to cast themselves resolutely as private citizens and independent entrepreneurs."[6] Having withdrawn from the terrible realities of contemporary life, such writers offer fiction that "suffers from a reduced authority."[7] Although he does not cite Philip Roth's well-known writer's lament concerning American reality—"it stupefies, it sickens, it infuriates, and finally it is even a kind of embarrassment to one's meager imagination"[8]—he nevertheless recognizes the same dilemma. But whether in fleeing that world writers turn inward, exquisitely anatomizing the most minute rhythms of private life, or whether they turn outward in a dazzling display of postmodernist artistry, novelists "may be failing the task."[9] Both misdirections of creative energy can derive from the same cause; "the coercion of *Realpolitik,* the ideology of cold war and the shadow of the bomb may have robbed us of the passion of our calling, which is the belief that writing matters, that there is salvation in witness and moral assignment."[10] However one judges Doctorow's fiction, it is clear that he has not dodged such issues in his own work.

As a consequence of his commitment to the calling, Doctorow's novels since *The Book of Daniel* have been a frequent source of controversy. This often bitter discussion has been generated, not by the writer's experimental techniques but rather by the ostensible politics of his fiction. *Daniel* has been seen by many critics—hostile and admiring alike—as a partisan treatment of the old and new left and as an attempt to exonerate condemned atomic spies Julius and Ethel Rosenberg while indicting both the American culture of their time and ours. *Ragtime* and *Loon Lake* have also been charged with, or praised for, what is seen as their negative critical assessments of the country's past and present. Conservative critics such as Hilton Kramer, Pearl Bell, Robert Alter, and Joseph Epstein have based their attacks on the issue of Doctorow's alleged membership in what Epstein calls the "adversary culture," a constituency originally described by Lionel Trilling. The writer's emancipation from the establishment, Trilling wrote, was widely thought necessary and possible in order to "liberate the individual from the tyranny of his culture" so that he might be able "to stand beyond it in an autonomy of perception and judgment." Epstein uses Trilling's description to excoriate not only Robert Coover's outrageous novel *The Public Burning*, but also Doctorow's *The Book of Daniel*, as well as to condemn those elements in academia believed to have fostered this attitude through a "bitter [educational] diet of literary modernism and the tradition of alienation from their country."[11] Epstein believes that "at the bone Doctorow is a writer of the adversary culture," one of that by now large group of Americans who have developed "an intense distrust of [this] country that borders on hatred."[12] Epstein concludes his essay with the suggestion—especially absurd when applied to Doctorow—that such novelists are "glad to tap dance in the rubble of history."[13]

Doctorow would, however, surely embrace Trilling's description of the writer's necessary autonomy—he conceives of such a group of artists as composing "a kind of democracy of perception" (*DOP,* 184)—and, on the face of it, his fiction could clearly be called adversarial. The issues raised by these critics, however, can be reduced to a single premise: to them the writer who stands outside his culture and uses that position to criticize those aspects, political or social, that his judgment calls into question, is automatically against, and therefore an enemy of, the culture. Such a position has led these critics and reviewers grossly to misread Doctorow's complex and deeply ambiguous fiction, fiction never amenable to any simple social analysis. This either/or position, moreover, is matched in many ways by another set of critics coming from the left, those whose similar fixation with political judgments constantly distorts their analysis of Doctorow's work by reducing its focus to those social issues that they themselves warmly endorse.[14] Although admiring critics of the left typically have had more useful things to say about

Doctorow's art, it nonetheless seems to be the *subject* of Doctorow's fiction, more than its *treatment,* that preoccupies both groups of critics.

"The Wisdom of Uncertainty"

Doctorow would agree with Toni Morrison who, as a black, is one of those American writers who necessarily assumes the political significance of fiction: "I am not interested in indulging myself in some private, closed exercise of my imagination," she says; if fiction has no political significance "it is tainted."[15] Doctorow cites the social topics and themes of past fiction and acknowledges that he shares such concerns with earlier writers. He believes, in fact, that it is "hard to think of a writer who cannot be given a very rigorous political interpretation" (*EC,* 60), and when pressed by an interviewer whose interest is obviously political, he can admit that his is "a poetics of engagement" (*EC,* 48), no doubt made more inevitable by his identification with immigrants. But when urged to acknowledge a specific political theme in *Loon Lake,* Doctorow flatly asserts his priorities: "Novelists are not politicians."[16] "To think that I'm writing to advance a political program," he argues, "misses the point. To call a novel political today is to label it, and to label it is to refuse to deal with what it does. My premise is that the language of politics can't accommodate the complexity of fiction, which as a mode of thought is intuitive, metaphysical, mythic."[17] By the same token, he recognizes that here is a "kind of death that creeps into prose when you're trying to illustrate a principle, no matter how worthy" (*EC,* 60). His conviction is thus like that asserted by Michael G. Cooke: art approaches universality "when it conveys conviction and yet recalls that all mere dogmas are linked to death as their origin and end."[18]

Ideologues, Milan Kundera has pointed out, seek the "either-or"; unable "to tolerate the essential relativity of things human" they are thus unable to accept "the novel's . . . wisdom of uncertainty."[19] Doctorow himself asserts that good fiction, no matter how strenuous its social commitment, must "usually end up acknowledging, by its very nature, the ambiguities" (*EC,* 49) of its subject. Thus, like the vast majority of contemporary writers, Doctorow continually demonstrates the classic modern preference for exploration and discovery over thesis; in describing his activity in the composition of *World's Fair* as "writing to find out what I was writing,"[20] he repeats a claim he has made often throughout his career. Far from approaching his novels as vehicles for dramatizing political convictions, he emphasizes the accidental way each has been initiated. And asked whether he brings a preconceived notion to a novel's creation, Doctorow draws an interesting analogy: his manner of composition is "not a terribly rational way to work," he admits, "It's hard to explain . . . it's like driving a car at night. You never see further than your headlights, but you can make the whole trip that way."[21] The novelist begins and, sometimes, ends in uncertainty.

Such tentativeness in no way diminishes the novelist's concern, since "good fiction is interested in the moral fate of its people" (EC, 40). Doctorow has tacitly endorsed the label "Radical Jewish Humanist" (EC, 53–54) and he has acknowledged being, in American terms, a leftist "of the pragmatic, social democratic left—the humanist left that's wary of ideological fervor" (EC, 52). He has on occasion, moreover, tentatively acknowledged his support for some qualified and indigenous form of American socialism, although at least once he described, with his characteristic skepticism, the "exhaustion" of "twentieth-century political alternatives"; "capitalism, communism, socialism . . . none of it seems to work" (EC, 65). When asked to summarize his social ideals, he replied simply, "There is a presumption of universality to the ideal of justice—social justice, economic justice. And it's a Platonic ideal too—that everyone be able to live as he or she is endowed to live; that if a person is in his genes a poet, he be able to practice his poetry. Plato defined justice as the fulfillment of a person's truest self" (EC, 55).

Inventing the Past

Given Doctorow's social and political convictions, it is not surprising to discover that in one way or another, all of his novels make use of American history: the expansion of the West in *Welcome to Hard Times,* the forties, fifties and sixties in *The Book of Daniel,* the first fifteen years of this century in *Ragtime,* the Great Depression in *Loon Lake* and *World's Fair.* On this score *Ragtime* in particular has elicited much discussion, since in that novel Doctorow not only repeatedly invokes history by employing actual events but, more importantly, he fictionalizes a number of historical personages in unverifiable ways, often doing violence to our sense of their actual roles. The discussion of this element in his work has become a major critical commonplace in reviews, analyses, and interviews and will emerge at various points in the following chapters. Doctorow's manipulation of history has delighted many readers but annoyed some who distrust what they believe to be the resulting distortion of past reality.

Doctorow is only one of many contemporary novelists who make various uses of historical materials; Gore Vidal, William Styron, Norman Mailer, Thomas Pynchon, John Barth and Robert Coover, to mention only a few, have all exploited the possibilities for redefining the nature of the past. Nor are these writers the first to do so; the many manifestations of the historical novel can be traced back through the history of the genre. In particular, the publication of *Ragtime* brought immediately to the minds of many readers John Dos Passos's ambitious trilogy, *U.S.A.* But as Barbara Foley points out, whereas Dos Passos "frames his narrative around facts which are ordinarily held to be 'true,' in the sense that they are externally verifiable," Doctorow "treats with equal aplomb facts that are 'true' and those that are 'created,' thus calling into question our concept of factuality and, indeed, of history itself" (*EC,* 168).

Doctorow has repeatedly justified this imaginative manipulation of the past, arguing again and again that "all history is composed" (*EC,* 43). His most extensive discussion of this view can be found in his seminal (if not fully consistent) essay "False Documents." In this piece he either elevates the novelist or lowers the historian, merging their tasks and identity: "What is an historical fact? . . . If it is to reach anyone else it is transmitted in words or on film and it becomes an image . . . History shares with fiction a mode of mediating the world for the purpose of introducing meaning, and it is the cultural authority from which they both derive that illuminates those facts so that they can be perceived. Facts are the images of history, just as images are the data of fiction" (*EC,* 24). Because history and fiction are both the products of the mediating imagination, Doctorow believes that he can "claim that history is a kind of fiction in which we live and hope to survive, and fiction is a kind of speculative history, perhaps a superhistory, by which the available data for the composition is seen to be greater and more various in its sources than the historian supposes." He is "thus led to the proposition that there is no fiction or nonfiction as we commonly understand the distinction: there is only narrative" (*EC,* 25, 26). Novelists, therefore, have the ability "to compose false documents more valid, more real, more truthful than the 'true' documents of the politicians or the journalists or the psychologists" (*EC,* 26); if such is the case, "history belongs more to the novelists and the poets than it does to the social scientist. At least we admit that we lie" (*EC,* 67). This position has allowed him to argue on several occasions, for example, that his invented story of J. P. Morgan and Henry Ford in *Ragtime* is "true, whether it happened or not" (*EC,* 69), and if his claim seems excessive, we may remind ourselves that as T. S. Eliot has written in his poem "Gerontion," history itself, with its "many cunning passages, contrived corridors / And issues, deceives with whispering ambitions, / Guides by vanities" (ll. 34–36).

At any rate, Doctorow recognizes that his is clearly "a novelist's proposition" (*EC,* 26), though in its frequent and sometimes bald repetition the presumably metaphorical nature of his argument seems, at times, to have literal force. And even when taken figuratively, one might ponder Barbara Foley's concern: "What I ultimately find disturbing about *Ragtime* . . . is its underlying postulate that whatever coherence emerges from the represented historical world is attributable to the writer's power as teller of his story, with the result that the process of historical reconstruction itself, rather than what is being represented, comes to the fore. 'Once History inhabits a crazy house,' writes Mailer, 'egotism may be the last tool left to History' " (*EC,* 175). Doctorow acknowledges that "there's a danger in this sort of thing," but he trusts that, taken collectively, writers as "independent witnesses" (*EC,* 69)—and thus not accountable to any institutional power—can, through the moral imagination, define the truth.

From Social Significance to Cosmic Implication

Asked by an interviewer whether he agrees with Freud's judgment in *Ragtime* that "America is a mistake, a gigantic mistake," Doctorow describes the passage as a kind of joke and concludes by adding "but I don't agree, of course, any more than I agree that any other nation is a mistake. They're all mistakes. Human life is a mistake" (*EC,* 57). The subject is dropped in the interview, and we can only guess how seriously Doctorow intended this comment to be taken. This incident offers, nonetheless, a kind of symbolism, for in the passage from which this excerpt is drawn, Doctorow's point of reference moves swiftly from the question of social value (mistakes are made because of human error, but it is possible for human error to be corrected) to cosmic reality (which is beyond the scope of human correction): life is a mistake. Here, then, is the fundamental paradox in Doctorow's fiction: the intensely held social convictions of the man inevitably collide with the imaginative realizations of the artist.

Though Doctorow has often accepted, sometimes with emendations but always with good humor, the conclusions about his work drawn by various interviewers, on the occasion of those discussions he only suggests his fundamental assumptions (or what might be called his cosmic politics), and he has never extensively articulated them outside his fiction. He has, however, acknowledged the influence of his paternal grandfather's secular, rationalistic legacy. As a Jew, a humanist, and a radical, both directly and through Doctorow's father, his grandfather contributed to Doctorow's sense of human possibility and responsibility; "all the solutions were to be found right here on earth, and the supernatural was not taken seriously"[22]—a view most appropriate for the immigrant. Throughout Doctorow's essays and interviews one senses the power of this legacy: we *can,* we *must* do better. When he

was in his twenties he was, like many others of his generation, deeply influenced by existentialism, a philosophical point of view that he recognizes has
been strongly affected by European totalitarianism and the "monstrous society of death," of "hellish barbarism," that it produced—a "philosophical alienation" that led to a "brave recognition of an amoral universe." "I grew up
on Sartre and Camus and others like their predecessor Husserl," he says; "I
trust the existentialist vision." "Is it pessimistic?" he asks; "I don't think so. It
assumes the obligation to engage to construct a just world—at least as I read
it—on the chance that meaning and God can be found that way." "Ethics is
only a human invention" but "our sense of right and wrong is no less strong
for that" (*DOP*, 183). Thus contemporary thought has reinforced his grandfather's convictions and, as political man, Doctorow continues patiently to
prod a world that has not yet reached its human potential.

But the vision of the world actually implied by Doctorow's fiction is quite
another matter; here human possibility is continually frustrated, not simply
by man's political failures or even by human psychology, but by something in
the very nature of things: human life, it often seems, is a mistake. (It is everywhere apparent that the influences that have shaped Doctorow are European;
yet in his pessimistic view of the cosmos we are reminded that though he appears to have little interest in Emersonian idealism, he nonetheless has read
Melville, Hawthorne, and Poe with some care, having silently acknowledged
Melville's attribution to Hawthorne of "the power of blackness" as well as
Poe's "imp of the perverse.") Whether in the terrifying hopeful hopelessness
of Blue in *Welcome to Hard Times,* who grieves over his well-intended but
failed attempt to summon up out of the desolate prairie a civilization already
fatally doomed by the demonic Bad Man from Bodie, or in Daniel's terrible
realization of a universe where nothing connects in *The Book of Daniel,*
Doctorow's vision is repeatedly of a universe where meaninglessness and absurdity are at the center of things and lead to unending and inescapable repetitions of human failure. Even the historian Creighton in the least impressive
of Doctorow's books, the science fiction novel *Big As Life,* has "turned gray
trying to reconcile his natural optimistic nature with the dark depressing data
of his profession" (*Big as Life,* 12). Creighton's dilemma seems almost, but
not quite, to implicate Doctorow himself. Moreover, the question is no longer
one that Doctorow's grandfather might have pondered—how does the immigrant create a new American life?—but rather the dilemma of the cosmic
"immigrant, as in every moment of his life, arriving eternally on the shore of
his Self" (*Ragtime,* 368).

Although much criticism of Doctorow's fiction has understandably
concerned itself with his social views and his uses of history, a series of sig-

nificant essays have quietly pondered this bleak existential strain in his works. Whether, for example, it is Barbara Cooper's analysis of the images of endless repetition (which saturate his novels), David Emblidge's study of Doctorow's theme of illusory progress, or Herwig Friedl's complex theory of energy and entropy alternating in his work,[23] the novelist who emerges from such thoughtful discussions is not ultimately moved by social concerns but rather by a profoundly pessimistic view of the human condition located, it appears, in a world where the forces of good and evil repeatedly wax and wane, where life is followed only by death, where his grandfather's "obligation to . . . construct a just world" appears not only absurd but impossible, and where self-realization can never be fully achieved. Social analysis assumes not only the possibility of making sense out of history, but also the ability to discover those structures that more justly and humanely enable the realization of human potential. Yet, at the deepest level Doctorow's fiction seems to qualify or transcend the very social analysis that preoccupies so many of his readers.

"Glorious Noise"

Fortunately for the author and his readers, however, Doctorow's working concern is epistemological, not ontological, and the tension between his vision of meaningless repetition and his keen interest in human perception and creativity energizes, rather than weakens, his fiction. For if existentialism acknowledges no absolute, it yet sanctions, in Doctorow's wonderful phrase, "the creativity of man as a kind of glorious noise in the midst of silence" (*DOP*, 183). It is just this creative idealism and his belief in the moral imagination that convince him that "history is made; it's composed" (*DOP*, 184)—a conclusion fully compatible with his existential views.

Thus, if in most of his fiction Doctorow portrays a world in which human life is tragically problematic at both the social and cosmic levels, he nonetheless finds solace in perception and joy in creation. Without in the least betraying his social ideals, or his skeptical view of the world's potential, he recognizes that as an artist he owes primary allegiance to such interpretation of human experience as can be honestly invented. He has acknowledged that to some extent all of his books are "about writers of one sort or another, all of them are *Künstlerromane*" (*DOP*, 190). When asked whether artists incorporate all his interests or whether they are simply all he can write about, Doctorow answers "yes to both questions" (*DOP*, 191).

Thus in a novel such as *The Book of Daniel*, where the political significance looms so large, we find that "the novel's assertion of Daniel's growth signifies a triumph of art over ideology," as Sam B. Girgus points out, "Doctorow indicates his commitment to the world of imagination and creative coherence rather than to a restricted political doctrine of truth" (*DOP,* 88). Or, to put it in different terms, "thematic questions lead him to aesthetic ones" (*EC,* 75). In the last analysis, Doctorow writes a poetry of experience, rather than a poetry of assertion.

It is not, then, the political radical who interests Doctorow so much as the "little criminal of perception" (*Daniel,* 44) whose loyalty is always to his imagination. And it is not factual history that attracts the writer but rather the myth that many people unconsciously substitute for history and that is the obvious province of the artist. Hence, when Doctorow tells us that everything in *Ragtime* is "true," he means as true as the mythopoeic imagination can make it. Such a position places him in sharp opposition to traditional novelists for whom realism is the goal, and simultaneously sets him apart from the postmodernists whose fictional strategies he so frequently employs. Although like many of the latter writers he creates various devices that challenge verisimilitude and shatter the traditional novelist's illusion of concrete reality, his goal in so doing is quite different from theirs. Whereas John Barth's self-reflexivity, for instance, appears intended continually to remind the reader that he is participating in an aesthetic game that must not be confused with reality, Doctorow's similar manipulations are intended to convince the reader of complex states of being. Speaking of the multiple endings of *Daniel,* Dieter Schulz says that thus fiction "undercuts itself, not in the postmodernist sense of free play, but from an impulse to do justice to the complexity and elusiveness of history which defies whatever interpretive constructs one may impose upon it" (*DOP,* 16). And while in much of his work Barth seems to be attempting to disabuse the reader of older, Arnoldian assumptions about the value of creation and art, Doctorow's intention is clearly the reverse. The humanistic attempt to make sense out of an incoherent, meaningless and terrible reality—rather than to define a particular course of action or sport at its expense—is precisely the source of his belief in "the passion of our calling," which in the most basic terms is "the belief that writing matters, that there is salvation in witness and moral assignment."[24]

Thus the innovative and sophisticated fictional devices that we will see Doctorow continually employ from *Daniel* on are meant to return us to a complex reality—not to distance us from it; the artist uses all the strategies he can invent to control the absurd world through an artistic mastery of it; for in an absurd world the understanding achieved through art is the only control possible for the writer, whatever the activist's belief might be.

Chapter Two

"A Relentlessly Revisionist Spirit":
Welcome to Hard Times
and *Big as Life*

While many superb writers produce sophisticated novels at extraordinarily young ages—Fitzgerald published *The Great Gatsby* at twenty-nine, Hemingway *The Sun Also Rises* at twenty-eight, Faulkner *The Sound and the Fury* at thirty-two—it is rare for young writers to create novels with absolutely no autobiographical referrents or content. Fitzgerald, Hemingway, and Faulkner, as well as many contemporary novelists such as John Irving, Joyce Carol Oates, John Updike, Joan Didion, Richard Ford, Toni Morrison, John Gardner, Mary Gordon, Gail Godwin, Philip Roth, and even John Barth created their early works out of at least some of the threads of personal, frequently adolescent, experiences.

Unlike many of his predecessors and most of his contemporaries, however, the young Doctorow came to his vocation as a writer from an unusual apprenticeship; his considerable experience as a literary and film editor clearly affected his decision to abandon the inevitable autobiographical novel with which he was struggling in order to experiment with a genre—the western—he had been reading and critiquing for months: "I don't imagine I would have written *Welcome to Hard Times* if I'd not been working at that film company and reading lousy screenplays week after week" (*EC*, 33).

"*Not* Autobiographical Writing"

Welcome to Hard Times, published in 1960 when he was only twenty-nine, is therefore an unusual first work; it is a sparse, spare, and almost perfectly constructed novella with no trace of autobiographical content. Although clearly not as complex as *Ragtime* or *Loon Lake, Hard Times* is deceptively simple: more fable than story, more ballad or parable than traditional narrative, the sheer surface masks a far more opaque and ironic tale of life on the American frontier. And the book in no way pales beside

Doctorow's mature work, for it is a wholly self-contained, symmetrically structured, brilliantly narrated tour de force that presents a profound, if bleak, vision of experience—a vision that, however differently embodied in his later work, has informed Doctorow's entire literary career to date.

The experience of creating *Welcome to Hard Times* also taught Doctorow three seminal lessons about his artistic imagination and the creative process: "*Welcome to Hard Times* was crucial to me for a couple of reasons. First, because it showed me my strength, which was *not* autobiographical writing. Somehow I was the kind of writer who had to put myself through prisms to find the right light—I had to filter myself from my imagination in order to write. The second thing I learned was that all writing begins as accident" (*EC,* 34). And the third lesson was about the power of illusion: "from reading all these screenplays and being forced to think about the use of Western myth, I developed a kind of contrapuntal idea of what the West must really have been like. Finally one day I thought '*I* can lie better than these people' " (*EC,* 34).

A Contrapuntal Idea

The contrapuntal patterns of *Welcome to Hard Times* are indeed multiple. Beginning with an inverse image of what the popular imagination fantasized as the fertile land of opportunity, Doctorow created an arid, rocky, empty landscape bereft of life, of growth, and ultimately, of hope: "no trees out there. Jesus, that was beautiful. I could spin the whole book out of one image. And I did" (*EC,* 39).

Grounded in this starkest of landscapes, *Welcome to Hard Times* is structured in three major parts, each part representing one of the three ledgers kept by a man called, simply, Blue. Originally bequeathed by an entrepreneurial stagecoach driver so that Blue might keep the Express accounts of trade transactions in the tiny plains town of Hard Times,[1] the ledgers are transformed by Blue from record- and list-keeping devices to the paper on which he commits his and the town's doomed experience: Hard Times's "Bible." And each of the three ledgers represents almost precisely a third of the history of Hard Times, a history that Blue is writing retrospectively, after the town and its people have been twice destroyed. The symmetrical and symbolic arrangement of the ledgers—describing in turn destruction, creation, destruction—reflects simultaneously the primitive natural cycle, an existential, even nihilistic view of experience, and a deeply ironic inversion of the western myth.

Blue (sometimes called "Mayor," although he is never officially so elected) is a middle-aged man in the present of the novel (some twenty to thirty years after the Civil War[2]) who came West "with expectations of something, I don't know what" (7). At the age of forty-eight, having lost his wife some twenty years before, and having lived the peripatetic life of a rover moving "from one side of the West to the other" (29), Blue first comes to Hard Times on his meandering route to earn money in the gold mines in the hills north of the town. Settling there and quickly assuming responsibilities as the town recorder, Blue becomes de facto Mayor, incipient chamber of commerce promoter, budding capitalist, and community guru who delights in the building of the small town and in his unofficial place at its center.

Blue's narrative begins, however, with the story of the day the few occupants of the saloon watch a man named Clay Turner ride into town, get summarily drunk, rape, mutilate, plunder, murder, and eventually burn down the town during a few hours of orgiastic cruelty and barbarism, single-handedly creating a miniholocaust that is scandalously unchecked by most of the male citizens of the community. Finally satiated, "The Bad Man from Bodie" simply disappears while the few stunned survivors bury their dead or pack their wagons and seek other settlements somewhere in the vast Dakota territory. Left with Jimmy Fee, a boy Turner has just orphaned, Blue's only other companions are an apparently deaf-mute Indian named John Bear, and Molly Riordan, a whore, who presumably has been raped and left for dead in the rubble of the burned saloon. Nevertheless, undaunted, Blue quickly lays plans to remain and rebuild the hapless town.

Blue is soon aided in his efforts by the arrival of a troupe of immigrant women led by a Russian entrepreneur named Zar. Anxious to establish his bar and bordello in a town that currently boasts neither, Zar agrees to cater to the miners and begins the bartering processes that mark the most rudimentary acts of human beings engaged in developing societies. Blue soon persuades Zar and young Jimmy to accompany him to another burned-out town where they find lumber to initiate the literal rebuilding of the town once again appropriately named Hard Times.

A Lost Possibility

The middle, and most lyric, section of the novel recounts the rebuilding of the town and the gradual shaping of Blue's pathetic surrogate "family": "wife" Molly and "son" Jimmy Fee. This "Second Ledger" deftly and poetically embodies the reemergence of life and hope in the simplest and most familiar metaphors of creation and rebirth to conjure up the temporary illusion of well-being. For Blue admits: "A person cannot live without looking for good signs, you just cannot do it" (89).

The second ledger begins with Blue's description of Molly wearing a wedding dress given to her by one of Zar's whores and the cross she clutched earlier in her burned and comatose state. These crude symbols come to evoke both positive and ironic meanings as Blue and Molly do "marry" in a touching and simultaneously perverse way, and Molly does briefly bring him profound moments of happiness; but she also brings him pain, for she finds him lacking what to her is the simple manly courage he should have exhibited to defeat the Man from Bodie, so that he suffers her disdain.

While apparently nurturing the development of her "family," Molly begins the process of training Jimmy to reject Blue and his values and to become the engine of Turner's destruction once he inevitably returns to Hard Times. Suffering a traumatic winter together in the claustrophobic confines of their makeshift earthen dugout, not-so-subtle love-hate relationships slowly develop among the three. Blue nevertheless remains optimistic despite moments of despair when "if I thought about the spring it was as a lost possibility" (108).

But just as inevitably, the spring does come and signs of life abound everywhere in the town. Settlers of various immigrant backgrounds and types (often either physically or psychologically maimed) arrive and fledgling businesses thrive; Blue is in his element and Molly likewise appears to be softened by the prosperity: "There was a feeling of celebration in everything that was going on" (117).

Molly's Final Fool

As the Second Ledger ends, the signs of superficial success are abundant; a man from the office of the governor of the territory has left "Mayor" Blue a town charter and a petition for statehood, both of which seem to make manifest Blue's dream of creating the facsimile of a frontier civilization. But Doctorow never lets us rest in the complacency of the dream; the government man plays the role of a stark choric voice reminding Blue, and us, that towns need jails and a "shootist," and even so protected are ephemeral: "The claim pinches out, the grass dies, the well dries up, and everyone will ride off to form up again somewhere else for me to travel. Nothing fixes in this damned country, people blow around at the whiff of the wind" (142). Molly, too, senses annihilation, although from the more palpable source that is Clay Turner; in fact, she is both obsessed and despairing in her vain attempts to persuade Blue to leave Hard Times. He believes so totally in the protections of civilization, however, that he rejects Molly's pleadings in the illusion that "a settled town drives them away" (152).

Molly withdraws in a grim paranoia interrupted only by her attempts to cultivate the friendship of Jenks, the town's shootist and sheriff, her sole link to the real "manliness" (155) she believes has the power to thwart Clay Turner on his inevitable return. Nurturing Jimmy's admiration for Jenks, Molly turns their "son" against Blue who finally recognizes that "she was training him for the Bad Man, she was breaking him into a proper mount for her own ride to Hell" (162).

Attempting to maintain his optimism in the face of mounting evidence to the contrary, Blue increasingly becomes cognizant of the ambivalent nature of the town's teeming life and complexity; trouble is everywhere as the growing suspicion that the Eastern mining executives' promises of extensive gold mining and development are hollow promises indeed. But Blue cannot face the potential failure of his town, so in lieu of the wages they are vainly waiting to earn, he lends money to opportunists, attempts to mediate conflicts, and plays the role of a government under siege, placing every finger in the holes of the disintegrating dike. As the tension builds, Archie Brogan, the inscrutable mine foreman, having read a letter Blue assumes is from the Eastern owners of the mine, packs his saddlebags and leaves the town, signaling the end of the glory days and triggering a chaotic and looting migration out of Hard Times. Blue helplessly watches the end of his town, his raison d'être, and knows that "when it's too late we see what a fraud it is, what a poor pinched-out claim" (186), but is still utterly powerless to abandon his dream. And then, inevitably, he sees the reflection of Clay Turner in the mirror of Zar's all-but-empty saloon and savors the irony of his situation: "He never left the town, it was waiting only for the proper light to see him where he's been all the time" (198). Deciding he has nothing to lose by "becoming Molly's final fool" (205), Blue enlists a decent settler called simply "Swede" into a daring plot to trap and kill the Bad Man. Wounding Turner (who nevertheless kills Swede), Blue—in an uncharacteristic act of machismo—takes the insensible body to Molly and Jimmy as an awful gift to their obsession. But the Bad Man is not easy to kill, and in a macabre scene of ironic, even pagan, slaughter (in which Molly repeatedly knifes Turner's wounded body), Jimmy accidently shoots both Molly and Turner in their deathly embrace and wounds his "father" as Blue attempts to stave off the ultimate tragedy. The town is simultaneously looted and abandoned and Jimmy Fee rides off, the new incarnation of the Bad Man from Bodie, leaving Blue to finish his ledgers and die a broken man.

Inverted Western Myth

One of the most fascinating aspects of the critical discussion of *Welcome to Hard Times* is that the novel has engendered controversy of a surprising sort. That is, while one might anticipate the debate to focus on the literary value of the novel—some arguing that it is a thin, cliche-ridden and obvious allegory while others extol the fable-like qualities of its poetic economy—a substantial part of the discussion centers on the question of whether or not Doctorow successfully demythicizes the traditional western and thereby gives us a historically more accurate understanding of our heritage than the typical western novel or film did before 1960.[3] Indeed, some critics argue that the novel is a superbly effective embodiment of the true American spirit: capitalistic, brutally competitive, and selfish from the very inception of the pioneering efforts to settle the West. Those who hold this view tend to echo what Arthur Saltzman characterizes as the "relentlessly revisionist spirit [that] informs *Welcome to Hard Times*" (*EC,* 76) and therefore see the novel as nothing short of revolutionary in its original, and by implication, "true" treatment of the American West.[4] These same critics tend to see the novel as an antiwestern, as a debunking of the western as a romantic genre.

Others, notably Stephen L. Tanner, argue that Doctorow's nihilistic treatment of the West is nothing short of heretical, the result of his literal ignorance of the place and its history: "Doctorow has no appreciation . . . of the pleasure, beauty, and spiritual invigoration that the westerner's direct contact with a vast natural environment can produce, even when that environment is at times harsh and solitary. This blind spot in Doctorow's experience poisons the very spring of the book's conception."[5] Invoking the biographical fallacy with a vengeance, Tanner argues that Doctorow's real problem stems from his limited background: "It is easy to understand how a man living most of his life in New York City would be fascinated and repelled by the image of a vast, barren, uninhabited land,"[6] thereby concluding that *Welcome to Hard Times* is an example of "another unfortunate attempt to debunk the Western."[7]

The arguments in either direction tend to miss one of Doctorow's basic artistic premises—that history and myth, fact and fiction, are hopelessly and inextricably meshed together in a seamless fabric of the imagined and the "real." Whether or not *Hard Times* literally recaptures the "reality" of the American West is therefore less relevant than that it offers an alternative set of images and a compelling, original vision; as a literary construct, it radically revises our experience of both the genre and the myth of the American West, and that is its artistic triumph.

Historian As Artist

The key to *Welcome to Hard Times* is its narrator and his self-appointed task as keeper-of-the-records. Whatever view we develop of the West, whatever image we have of Hard Times and its fate, we have because Blue creates it for us. Even if we assume Blue's vision is a direct reflection of Doctorow's (and we will show how often other versions of that same vision emerge in his later work), Blue's is the sole, uninterrupted perspective through which we view the post–Civil War American West as it is embodied in one small town and in one attenuated period of time. No independent points of view or authorial intrusions serve to modify or mitigate Blue's vision, a vision that is initially the product of sometimes contradictory values and countervailing instincts; these values and instincts are ultimately identified in the novel with the paradoxically related values of history and art and the sometimes interchangeable—sometimes mutually excluding—visions of the historian and the artist, a tension repeatedly explored in Doctorow's fiction.

In an interesting study of *Welcome to Hard Times,* Marilyn Arnold argues that Blue, acting as recording historian, also shapes his story in such a way that it reinforces the very fatalistic conclusions he appears to draw from experience: "By seeing history as a pattern that has repeated itself and will continue to repeat itself, he ensures the repetition of that pattern" (*EC,* 208). If Arnold is right, the historian becomes the artist at the precise moment when he begins to shape the products of his observations and embue them with a particular vision, in this case, a fatalistic vision. A transcendent activity occurs—externally observed experience becomes the grist for the mill of the creative imagination. We are no longer in the realm of "objective reality" (whose very existence Doctorow repeatedly questions throughout his fiction), but in the province of art where imagined truth is the only meaningful truth. "There is no history," asserts Doctorow, "except as it is composed" (*EC,* 24). In the very process of composing the ledgers, therefore, the "truth" that Blue simultaneously *creates* and *perceives*—the fatalism that defines his and the town's experience—causes him to abandon what he has come to understand were his former illusions: "Nothing is ever buried, the earth rolls in its tracks, it never goes anywhere, it never changes, only the hope changes. . . . The first time I ran, the second time I stood up to him, but I failed both times, no matter what I've done it has failed" (214–15). Blue's former commitment to "progress" and to the salutory effects of civilization in the Enlightenment sense (so abundantly present in the views of those who historically civilized the West and wrote Rousseauesque accounts such as *The*

Pioneers and *The Virginian*[8]) is thereby destroyed. He never, however, utterly abandons hope or his very genuine humanity.

A Printed Circuit

Blue begins the serious job of writing the history of Hard Times after Turner destroys the town a second time and Blue himself is fatally wounded. The precise circumstances of Blue's decision to write the story, however, are not fully revealed until near the end of the novel. In other words, the real "present" of the novel is clearly identified only when Blue's account of the past merges with his immediate present, a present of seeming hopelessness and, it appears, imminent death. Paradoxically, Blue becomes cognizant too that "the closer I've come in time the less clear I am in my mind" (202–203), a recognition that "objectivity" may be possible only as a function of time and memory.

Throughout the narrative, however, Blue gradually, incrementally, reveals his motives for recording the history of Hard Times, motives that become increasingly complex as they are revealed and, it would seem, actually discovered by him.[9] From the earliest reference, "Now I'm trying to write what happened" (44), to "What I'm trying to do now is account for the way things went" (108), to the far more ambitious "Now I would write about that spring in its every minute if I could" (114), to the reflective, almost elegiac, "I have been trying to write what happened but it is hard, wishful work" (149), Blue moves—as he discovers the task of "writing what happened" to be a futile, if not impossible, one—to the profound, and ultimately artistic insight in which his effort culminates:

Of course now I put it down I can see that we were finished before we ever got started, our end was in our beginning. I am writing this and maybe it will be recovered and read . . . I scorn myself for a fool for all the bookkeeping I've done; as if notations in a ledger can fix life, as if some marks in a book can control things. There is only one record to keep and that's the one I'm writing now, across the red lines, over the old marks. It won't help me nor anyone I know. "This is who's dead," it says. It does nothing but it can add to the memory. The only hope I have now is that it will be read—and isn't that a final curse on me, that I still have hope? (187–88)

As he writes, Blue discovers not only the difficulty in replicating or embodying objective reality (of acting as "historian"), he also discovers that writing is, by its very nature, an act of hope and of life. He knows now that the act of the record keeper, the historian, cannot "fix life," cannot "control things." The "only record to keep" is the one he is writing now—the imaginative (fictive) record that may be read. In this sense, Blue discovers the literary raison d'être that Doctorow so succinctly describes in his essay "False Documents": "Fiction is a not entirely rational means of discourse. It gives to the reader something more than information. Complex understandings, indirect, intuitive, and nonverbal, arise from the words of the story, and by a ritual transaction between reader and writer, instructive emotion is generated in the reader from the illusion of suffering an experience not his own. A novel is a printed circuit through which flows the force of a reader's own life" (*EC,* 16).

As he writes, what Blue calls elsewhere his "stupid hope" evolves into the hope of creating the "ritual transaction" between himself and a possible reader, the "printed circuit" that links his life and experience to that of another (anonymous) human being. To affect that end, Blue reaches out to a potential reader, comfortable in "a stuffed chair with a rug under him and a solid house around him" at whom he rails: "Do you think, mister, with all that settlement around you that you're freer than me to make your fate?" (187). To create the "ritual transaction," Blue, like T. S. Eliot and Baudelaire before him, summons up his own "hypocrite lecteur," one who, by the force of this narrative, will be touched and share what is otherwise the wrenchingly lonely and isolated experience of Blue's life. In this final desire to generate the connecting "circuit" through his story,[10] Blue is, purely and simply, the artist.

A Regime Language

The raw material of literature is, of course, language. Talk is one of the special activities in which Blue frequently and strategically engages from the very beginning of his tenure in Hard Times. Moreover, he uses language as both a tool and a weapon throughout the novel. This facility with language is unusual in Hard Times because many members of the community are either not native speakers of American English or are men and women of action rather than words. But Doctorow uses the presence or absence of language for symbolic purposes rather than merely to suggest the stereotypical view of the strong and silent pioneering spirit of the nonintellectual men and women of the frontier. Few noble savages or settlers exist here.

On the one hand, silence connotes a profound mistrust of civilization and a refusal to communicate with it, as in the figure of the allegedly deaf-mute Indian, John Bear. In his case, silence in no way symbolizes lack of sensitivity, however, for John Bear is a natural healer (curing both Molly of her burns and Jimmy of pneumonia), and is likewise more at one with the land—as his pathetic garden attests—than is any other member of this community of nonproductive entrepreneurs. His inarticulateness, however, does limit his ability to function in civilization and he lives on the margins—both of the community and of self-realization—for apart from his natural skills, he is every bit as isolated in Hard Times as any of the nonnative settlers and finds his only mission in life the revenge he ultimately extracts from Zar for an earlier insult. Even this vestige of "natural man" is consumed by a destructive passion that manifests itself in murder by scalping, an Indian version of the murders committed by white men in this dying community.

The Bad Man from Bodie, Clay Turner, is another character who speaks few words in either of his debauching stays in Hard Times. Demonic laughter, a few intimidating commands or insults, and an occasional brutish grunt are the only expressions he musters, other than the deadly ones he inflicts with purely physical force.

And like his real mentor, Turner, Jimmy Fee eschews words; he exchanges the reading lessons Blue offers from the almanac for lessons in marksmanship and gun care provided by Jenks, another hopelessly inarticulate character whose few words reflect a pathetically small mental capacity to deal with his job as town protector and official record keeper. Indeed, his failure to understand the uses and power of language is made embarrassingly obvious on two critical occasions—first when he quickly transfers back to Blue the recordkeeping and letter writing responsibilities he acquired on being named Sheriff, because at least Blue "knew how to write" (144); and, even more dramatically, when Molly, with hypocritical sweet talk, apparently offers him irresistible delights in exchange for a foolhardy promise to shoot Turner. Jenks dies an ignoble death, taking "a clown's tumble down the steps" (206) because "the wolfy fool licked the syrup of [Molly's] words" (203). The pattern is clear: men who cannot use or understand the uses of language (and who are described in animal terms) choose instead the language of the regime—the gun (or the scalping knife).

In "False Documents" Doctorow draws this distinction: "There is a regime language that derives its strength from what we are supposed to be and a language of freedom whose power consists in what we threaten to become" (*EC,* 17). In the case of men in Blue's American West, that "regime language" is physical or brute force. In the case of the women of Hard Times, particularly Molly, that language is the language of sexuality, meagerly given (for a price), or sold. Blue comes to learn in the course of telling his story that the language and experience of the regime is cyclical, fatalistic, hopeless; but he also learns to use and explore the "language of freedom," the language of art. That language leads, against all evidence to the contrary, to hope, to the belief in community and life—indeed to Blue's last, but absolutely critical act and the narrative's last line; he refuses finally to set the ruined town afire because "I have to allow, with great shame, I keep thinking someone will come by sometime who will want to use the wood" (215).

This stubborn and utterly unwarranted optimism is ultimately a function of the creative act itself and points back to other creative acts; Blue's early use of the wood from a partially burned out town is a parallel act to his storytelling—both recreate Hard Times, one literally, the other figuratively. The "language of freedom," then, is the language of the artist that transcends "what we are supposed to be" and insists on "what we threaten to become," in this case the Sisyphean figure who will build communities from burned out cases despite the obvious futility of the endeavor.

However unlike one another Doctorow's novels are—and the diversity of his work is, as we have noted, one of his most remarkable and compelling qualities as a novelist[11]—the figure of the artist/historian and the transcendent nature of the creative act will continue to emerge. Although Blue is in many ways the clear prototype, analogous characters, often artist-narrators, abound. However dissimilar the manifestations, the voice of the artist struggling to discover—or, by an act of imaginative will, create—meaning is a constant presence in Doctorow's fiction. For Doctorow, perhaps more than for any of his contemporaries, the issues of who we are and how we know are often one and the same; his most successful works therefore inevitably explore the ontological through the epistemological and posit a fusion of the two. Unfortunately, unlike *Welcome to Hard Times,* his second novel fails to create that fusion and hence represents Doctorow's least arresting work.

Historian *and* Artist

Having experimented with the western with such precocious success in *Welcome to Hard Times,* Doctorow next focused his considerable imagination and skill on the other most formulaic of popular modes, science fiction, another subgenre of the novel. Created partly as parody, partly as serious social commentary, *Big as Life* remains for Doctorow something of an embarrassment. He "calls it 'a rather weak book,' and he won't allow it to be reprinted; hence, it remains his only work that is currently out of print."[12] Describing the novel as "unquestionably . . . the worst I've done" (*EC,* 37), Doctorow even goes so far as to compare it to another interesting failure: "I think about going back and redoing it some day, but the whole experience was so unhappy, both the writing and the publishing of it, that maybe I never will. It's my *Mardi*" (*EC,* 37), he observes, referring to Melville's third novel, a labored allegory rarely read.

Indeed, the unhappy experience of publishing this novel apparently led Doctorow to switch publishers for his third novel, for although his recent comments acknowledge the problems with *Big as Life,* he apparently had more faith in its value immediately after its creation: " 'There are some good things in that book, but it didn't work. Norman Mailer [for whom Doctorow served as editor while at Dial] once told me I didn't go far enough in that book, and I think he's right. I overcontrolled it.' " That, at least, is what Mr. Doctorow says now. At the time, he was enough of a writer to believe in his book and enough of an editor to see that his publisher, Simon & Schuster, didn't, which led him to change publishers.[13]

Whatever its flaws—and Doctorow's current assessment is basically accurate, if harsh—*Big as Life* is, nevertheless, interesting from several points of view. It is his only novel that does not, in whole or part, focus on some aspect of the American past; and, because it is told in a straightforward third-person narrative, as Paul Levine suggests, it does not offer "a distinctive narrative voice."[14] As Doctorow himself points out, *Big as Life* lacks precisely the characteristic that his more satisfying novels incorporate into their structures: "There are always characters in the books who do the writing. . . . I like to create the artist and let the artist do the work."[15]

Despite Doctorow's disclaimer, there *is* an artist in *Big as Life,* but he is not the character who does the writing. What Doctorow had done so successfully in *Welcome to Hard Times* he fails to do in his second novel. In Blue, Doctorow fused the figures of historian and artist in a single consciousness engaging in a struggle with itself. At the point when he discovers that language cannot replicate experience, and memory and externally observed reality can never be as one, Blue the artist transcends Blue the historian. In *Big as Life,* on the other hand, the paradox of historian/artist is ineffectual because it always remains bifurcated: two parallel characters, Red Bloom, a jazz musician, and Wallace Creighton, a professor of history, represent the parallel experiences of an artist and a historian in the face of an apocalyptic event analagous to the destruction of Hard Times. And while their lives and experiences intersect, the forces and instincts the two characters represent are never integrated or merged into a meaningful vision. The difference is absolutely critical to the success of *Welcome to Hard Times* and to the failure of *Big as Life,* for artistic and thematic closure occurs in Doctorow's first novel, while his second ends without any satisfactory thematic resolution.

This failure may well be a result, at least in part, of his choice to use the omniscient perspective to narrate his story. He originally made that same choice when he began *The Book of Daniel,* only to abandon it when he consciously or unconsciously discovered its limitations: "I can tell you that I started to write the book [*Daniel*] in the third person, more or less as a standard, past tense, third person novel, very chronologically scrupulous. . . . That moment, when I threw out those pages and hit bottom, was when I became reckless enough to find the voice of the book, which was Daniel" (*EC,* 62). Finding "the voice" then becomes the discovery that leads Doctorow to create his most memorable fiction. What he could not achieve in *Big as Life,* where there is no "voice," he achieves brilliantly in *The Book of Daniel* and, we will argue, in all his most successful work to date.

Chapter Three

"The Contingency of Song":
The Book of Daniel

As we have earlier noted, before fully committing himself to the writing of fiction, Doctorow had been immersed in the publishing world and thus had been "generically" educated; his transformation of the American western in *Welcome to Hard Times* and his use of science fiction in *Big as Life* represent his awareness of the potential in these two modes. At the outset of his career he had chosen forms of popular fiction that by their very nature could command large reading audiences. The seriousness and thematic rigor of these books, however, suggest that he certainly had more than commercial success in mind; both modes offer ways of looking at the American world that are at once familiar and yet susceptible to reinterpretation.

In his next novel Doctorow continued what has come to be his hallmark: the refusal simply to repeat fictional modes, however successful. Thus the brilliant *The Book of Daniel*, published in 1971, is a significant departure from his earlier work. After his innovative use of two popular forms, he chose to employ those very aspects of the modernist tradition that most challenge the expectations of readers of both popular and serious traditional fiction, the shattering of narrative line and the manipulation and fragmenting of the single narrative perspective into multiple points of view.

Daniel's Book

The four sections of Doctorow's third novel—"Memorial Day," "Halloween," "Starfish," and "Christmas"—consist of a tortured narrative by Daniel Lewin, son of tried and executed atomic spies Rochelle and Paul Isaacson, later adopted by decent, middle-class liberals. Twenty-five years old in 1967, living amid the social and ideological upheavals of the counterculture and New Left politics, Daniel attempts to make sense of his family past so that he can somehow understand the present and thus discover his own identity. Supposedly writing his doctoral dissertation at Columbia University during a time of great political instability, Daniel—using several largely nonscholarly narrational devices and, in part, identifying himself with the biblical prophet—actually describes the arrest, trial, and execution of his Communist parents during his childhood; the pathos of his and his sister Susan's life during and after these events; his sister's attempted suicide and ultimate death; and his own relentless attempts to uncover, analyze, and understand the dynamics of his painful past. Daniel interprets the "prevailing dreams of his society," Doctorow says, "and in the act of interpretation, his book, he manages to survive, where his sister does not" (*DOP,* 192).

Daniel starts his story in the present and includes such contemporary materials as the 1967 march on the Pentagon, but quickly and continuously the book recalls materials from the public and private past, primarily from the cold war era of his parents' prosecution and death. Two major time lines, then, are followed and conflated; his parents' world of the 1940s and 1950s and his own new age of the 1960s. Both mingle the personal and the public, the psychological and the political; cause and effect and logical parallels are at stake. There is progression in these simultaneous narratives and a sense of inevitable outcome, but each continually qualifies the other, and he can present neither in a linear sequence, because the primary focus of the novel is on the manner and limits of Daniel's knowing, not on the known. The contemporary narrative that opens and closes the novel ends with Daniel's provisional understanding, not so much of the historical reality of his family's past— neither their guilt nor innocence can be confirmed—but of himself, and includes the fragmented chronicle of pain that stimulates the modern story in the first place.

Since they were obviously minor party members and since the FBI can produce no very significant evidence against them, the Isaacsons' arrest for attempted treason and their subsequent trial for conspiracy suggests that callous political pressures may have produced a tragic miscarriage of justice. As most of the novel's readers recognize, their story bears some resemblance to the Ethel and Julius Rosenberg case, the degree of resemblance depending on how one judges the truth of the historical model. The Rosenbergs belonged, generally speaking, to the same ethnic and cultural ethos as that created by Doctorow for the Isaacsons; each family had two children (both boys in the historical case) and the Rosenberg sons, also subsequently adopted, eventually wrote a book published four years after Doctorow's novel and intended to exonerate their parents and indict American society and justice.[1]

Certainly Daniel is deeply concerned about his parents' guilt or innocence, and elements of the novel's plot can be traced to the circumstances of the historical trial and to the major controversy it created in the United States and elsewhere. Doctorow's novel has thus been occasionally compared to Robert

Coover's 1977 novel *The Public Burning,* a book that, for all its grotesque distortion of the Rosenberg materials, nonetheless directly mirrors their case. No such close connections should be made here. It must be emphasized that the plot as we have described it is not really derived from the Rosenberg case; Doctorow does not attempt either to represent it accurately or to determine where the historical truth of the case lies. The novel is not even the Isaacsons'; rather it is Daniel's own book—in much the same way that Conrad's *Heart of Darkness* is Marlow's and not Kurtz's.

"The Matter in My Heart": Perception, Prophecy, and Politics

At the heart of *The Book of Daniel* is a deep, radical trauma, the pain of dispossession, denial, abandonment—by parents, by friends, by country— the agony of familial destruction and death. It is a classically modern story of loneliness, alienation, and guilt, yet the ancient story, too, of the lost child and his mysterious birthright. It is a story about "the children of trials" (291) and therefore the trials of children. Whatever the reader's convictions concerning the festering wound of the counterculture or the cold war to which it is linked in this novel, that trauma is at the heart of Daniel's narrative; thus it is frequently a deeply moving book.

Against this trauma Daniel's sister Susan arms herself in a madness that allows her to withdraw from the pain into her "starfish" state (a life without consciousness somewhat like that for which Prufrock longed when he states he should have been "a pair of ragged claws / Scuttling across the floors of silent seas"). The starfish, an ancient sign suggesting "serenity and harmony with the universe" is now, Daniel notes, associated with bad luck. "This is undoubtedly because modern man can conceive of nothing more frightening than the self-sufficiency of being of the beautiful Starfish," Daniel argues; "he mistakes it for death" (267). But Daniel is either ironic or defensive here; if life is consciousness and hence identity, as the entire novel would seem to suggest, then such retreat, however understandable or serene, *is* death, while Daniel's own terrible compulsion to know (as a "criminal of perception," [291] the term he repeatedly uses for himself) is nonetheless life—however painful. Like Susan, Daniel, too, is very disturbed, and the condition of the children symbolically reveals the condition of the age. Daniel, however, is driven, not to madness but to its close ally, prophecy. Therefore, above all else, the novel becomes "the book of Daniel"—a vision that, of course, is what prophecy actually is. It is important, as we will see, to define Daniel's prophecy as a vision of the way things are and what has made them so, not as a prediction of the future or as a tribal remonstrance; he sets out neither to warn nor to threaten—surely not to achieve actual change in any sense. Nor, as prophet, does he write the book as a simple family partisan—any more than Doctorow writes simply as a political partisan in the Isaacson-Rosenberg case, though it may seem so at the outset. We can therefore disagree with the ostensible politics of this novel but, reading closely, we cannot escape Daniel's dilemma at the experiential level—the purely human agony of his prophecy. Daniel is on trial in this book, not his parents.

But if our primary response to the novel is to be moved by the narrator's experience, we should yet be aware of the enormously complex, often brilliant (if not always fully effective), literary technique through which Daniel's experience manifests itself. This novel has received high praise and great abuse, both too often in reaction to its perceived social vision. There is a large group of supportive critics who appear to admire the writer primarily for his social values. At any rate, its most vehement detractors have come from conservative circles, and they seem even more willing to ignore the novel qua novel than do many of its admirers.[2] Yet clearly this novel is, technically speaking, one of Doctorow's most ambitious books.

The book's opening pages establish a 1967–68 story and milieu. Daniel and his wife Phyllis are dressed in obligatory hippie uniform; language and description are immediately charged (casually and indirectly, but clearly) with social, economic and political innuendo; we hear of big cars, tawdry commercial life, implied social victimization, "enlightened liberals," "American flags . . . everywhere" (15). The book clearly evokes a very specific and predictable context. It commences with Daniel and Phyllis on their way to see Susan, who has been committed to an asylum after an attempted suicide. Worcester State Hospital may be seen as an opening metaphor for the state of the country in the late 1960s, just as in the novel's climax Disneyland can be viewed as the national asylum, or a sort of shrine to national senility.

But the early pages of the novel, with their accurate sociological and physical detail, at once mingle references to the biblical Daniel and his role as prophet; it is "Daniel, a Beacon of Faith in a Time of Persecution" (15) with whom the novel's Daniel identifies. Yet it is the prophet's "enigmas" and "weird dreams" (15) that attract him—the visionary, not the political Daniel. This mixture of biblical imagination and social reportage suggests something of the novel's strange blend of the didactic and the purely exploratory. Such fusion is characteristic of Doctorow's fiction in general, arguably didactic yet always ultimately following the logic of perception and imagination. Daniel, a self-confessed "criminal of perception," more nearly pursues

his own identity than his parents' innocence, though many reviewers have ignored that fact. The materials of biblical prophecy to which Doctorow alludes, of course, obviously suggest political parallels, but such passages have
only a vague and general application to his novel, especially as he employs
them, and have more to do with the creative, visionary side of his protagonist's life than with sociopolitical realities. The general effect of this pervasive
tension between social matter and personal vision is to energize the novel, to
produce a vivid sense of life and action. The immediate result is thus a high
level of reader interest, though there are also at times accompanying difficulties with narrative experimentation and hence, coherence.

The novel begins in the third person and shifts at once to first, then back to
third person—thus establishing the book's fluctuating narrative pattern,
and this third/first juxtaposition roughly parallels the sociopolitical/
visionary dichotomy of the novel. When successful, the effect of such experimentation with point of view is immediately to qualify the ostensibly social
aims of the book; from the outset our attention is increasingly drawn to the
perceiver and his perception, to the act of creation, to the storytelling process,
as opposed to the political issues. It is significant that Doctorow spent six
months and 150 pages on a straightforward narrative rendition of the story
and threw them away in disgust; they were, he said, "terrible, awful." When
he started again, it was because he recognized that "it had to be done in
Daniel's voice" (*EC*, 34–35), not his own. Daniel's book, in other words, had
to be a "false document" in order to tell the truth. The fact that Daniel immediately resorts to a kind of self-reflexivity ("The way to start may be," "how
would I get this scene to record?", "how do I establish sympathy?" [16]) reminds us that Doctorow finds the fictional devices and interests of the postmodernists attractive, that he too, like Daniel, is a "criminal of perception,"
(a term that perhaps also implies Doctorow's own ambivalence where questions of didacticism versus exploration are concerned).

Discussing the inevitable ambiguity at the heart of criminal trials—even
though trials are designed to resolve doubt—Doctorow says that "the most
important trials in our history, those which reverberate in our lives and have
most meaning for our future, are those in which the judgment is called into
question: Scopes, Sacco and Vanzetti, the Rosenbergs. Facts are buried, ex-
humed, deposed, contradicted, recanted. There is a decision by the jury and,
when the historical and prejudicial context of the decision is examined, a subsequent judgment by history. And the trial shimmers forever with just that
perplexing ambiguity characteristic of a true novel" (*EC*, 23). Doctorow was
not speaking directly about *The Book of Daniel* here, yet the observation is il-
luminating. The novel is certainly not "about" the historical Rosenbergs, and

it is not even primarily about the fictional Isaacsons; it does, however, shimmer with that perplexing ambiguity characteristic of a true novel. Doctorow's fiction is that the novel's author is Daniel himself, and the most common critical failure has been to deny or ignore the novel's central human experience: Daniel living *his* trial; writing—or rather struggling to write—*his* book. Daniel's book is an almost perfect example of Doctorow's theory of "false documents" discussed in chapter 1, a text in which the power and authority come from its very creation by someone other than the novelist. In Geoffrey Galt Harpham's words, Doctorow's novel (as opposed to Daniel's) "concerns the difficulties of a would-be narrator trying to turn a real event into a narrated one."[3]

Barbara L. Estrin, describing Daniel and his fellow "criminal of perception" Linda Mindish, points out that they both "survive without changing the world" (*EC,* 202), and David Gross, on the other hand, identifies the criminal of perception with the "radical writer or intellectual or political activist" (*EC,* 138). But this literalism misses the point of the existential rather than political "criminality" (and survival)—Daniel is the artist-as-subversive, not the radical-as-subversive. It is appropriate that Daniel, listing some of the more infamous American traitors, claims that "historians of early America fail to mention the archetypal traitor, the master subversive Poe, who wore a hole into the parchment and let the darkness pour through" (193). It was this antirationalist and anti-Emersonian whose demonic genius corroded American idealism: "It's Poe who ruined us, that scream from the smiling face of America" (194). On the face of it, Gross's description of Doctorow's technical innovation as a "maze of Modernist distancing strategies—which almost seem designed to protect him from the impact on us of his terrible vision" (*EC,* 147) is therefore a more promising idea; Doctorow himself has said that "presumptions of form tend to control presumptions of thought" (*Drinks,* xiv).

But if we examine Gross's assumption more closely, we realize that it obscures the almost involuntary nature of these epistemologically driven distortions of conventional narration, and we might easily reverse Doctorow's dictum: presumptions of thought tend to control presumptions of form. The question is, how should or can the artist know such a reality? Moreover, one might argue that what Gross interprets as Doctorow's innovative "distancing" is actually a reflection of the already "traditional," sometimes hackneyed, nature of these modernist devices in contemporary fiction. Thus if the book very much recalls the historical events and concerns of the 1950s and 1960s, it also reflects the Barthian directions taken during that period by some of fiction's most interesting practitioners. It needs to be emphasized that Doctorow, despite what has been called his radical Jewish-humanist background and its associated social commitment, can nevertheless not ignore the creative ferment of postmodernist relativism nor, more generally, art's profoundly existential appeal.

Daniel, at the book's outset, is discovered "searching, too late, for a thesis" (17), a problem that, in theory, Doctorow does not share, given his well-developed social and political convictions. But since, as we have earlier seen, he also believes that all texts, including versions of history itself, are fictional and freely create or discover their own meaning, discovery rather than statement becomes central here, "searching" is very much the issue. Thus, much of the author's energy at the book's outset and, indeed, throughout, goes into the creation of Daniel as artist figure. Whatever the social issues of Doctorow's third novel, as in its two predecessors, the protagonist here is overwhelmed by the need to sort out a reality so complex as to defy objective analysis; he can hope to understand only through an artist's act of the imagination, though Daniel never overtly identifies his work as much. Thus much, if not most, of the novel's fragmentary nature reflects Daniel's disturbed pursuit of the truth. Apparently random shifts in point of view and frequent dislocations of the narrative line both embody the disorderly process of Daniel's troubled thought and reflect various narrative strategies.

Appropriately, therefore, Doctorow has Daniel describe his biblical namesake as a prophet whose visions always tended toward the personal and the cryptic: "Toward the end [of his life] his insights become more diffuse, apocalyptic, hysterical" (22). And like his namesake, his need to understand his own perceptions became the biblical Daniel's burden: "I, Daniel, was grieved in my spirit in the midst of my body, and the vision of my head troubled me. . . . My cogitations much troubled me, and my countenance changed in me: but I kept the matter in my heart" (22). Doctorow's Daniel is also much troubled by his cogitations and, a few pages after this quotation from his namesake, he improvises on the private, therapeutic nature of such discovery: "IS IT SO TERRIBLE NOT TO KEEP THE MATTER IN MY HEART, TO GET THE MATTER OUT OF MY HEART, TO EMPTY MY HEART OF THIS MATTER? WHAT IS THE MATTER WITH MY HEART?" (27).

This eruption into bold print is the seventh and final item on a list of "subjects to be taken up" (26), matters concerning Daniel's present and past life that he thinks must be sorted out, understood, put into some kind of order so that he can reorganize his own identity. As in the case of the biblical Daniel's cogitations, the background of Daniel's personal crisis is public turmoil: "The summer of 1967 was just beginning. There would be a wave of draft-card burning. There would be riots in Newark and Detroit. Young people in the United States would . . . burn to death in protest" (27). But Daniel makes clear that however much he might respond to these events politically, he is first of all troubled by personal visions and he no longer wishes to—or perhaps can—keep the matter in his heart. Daniel's "book"—ostensibly his doctoral thesis, or his investigation of his past, or his confessional diary, or even his unacknowledged novel—offers him the chance to write his way out, to create, finally, the reality of his own existence and origins. Very late in the book Daniel refers to his attempt to reconstruct the past out of clues, distortions, and his own intuitions as "the novel as private I" (285). The metaphor and pun are telling, since they combine the crime-solving idea (and how many "criminals" there are here!) with a sense of the inevitably personal nature of knowledge—especially in the contemporary world. As the world and self are fragmented, so is the narrative.

Parents and Public

Yet Daniel's past has been unquestionably and inescapably politicized. Very early in the novel he plunges into an extended recollection of a critical moment in his childhood. The son of accused (and ultimately tried and executed) atomic spies, he and his sister Susan, whose mental breakdown opens the book, are taken to a huge rally in support of their indicted parents. Daniel and Susan are, of course, celebrities in their own right and the source of strong sentiment in the crowd. But they are, after all, only frightened and uncomprehending children; in this very effective scene they are dragged along by their parents' well-meaning lawyer, baffled by the nature of the event, used as psychological pawns in the social struggle. One passage makes clear their ambiguous position: " 'He's got the children!' they called to each other. Daniel could see a banner stretched on poles across the top of the platform ahead. FREE THEM! Someone lifted him up and he found himself being passed over the heads of the people, propelled sinuously like something on the top of the sea. He was terrified. He heard Susan's voice behind him. . . . 'Help! Danny!' " (32). They stare out at the crowd (to the little boy and girl "a vast hideous being of millions of eyes that seemed to undulate in the canyon of the street") and hear a sound "like the roar of the sea" (32). They are trapped at the crowd's center, much as are the imprisoned Isaacsons, much as they are trapped in the accident of their birth and life with their parents. They are trapped, too, in a set of conflicting values that demand their allegiance and punish those by whom it is withheld—socially and psychologically trapped by their legacy. The banner—"Free Them!"—suggests the ultimate irony.

The incident is crucial. Daniel writes his book in an attempt to free himself from the past, from his guilt over his parents' fate, from his guilt over his failure to save Susan, who finally succumbs to the family trauma—as well as to save himself and his own incipient family from the confusion and despair of the Isaacson legacy. The scene symbolizes the way that the public and the private, the present and the past, analysis and private vision—all mingle in the emerging exploratory process of *The Book of Daniel*. Later, when Doctorow mentions the presence of Norman Mailer and, especially, Robert Lowell at the Pentagon march, the peculiarly American theme of the private-public nature of literature is strongly invoked.

It is appropriate that Daniel should report on the effect of being a child of the Isaacsons before showing us the parents themselves; the complicated impact and legacy is indisputable, if unclear. When the parents begin to emerge in Daniel's commentary, as he pushes the chronicle backwards, they emerge as more complicated and ambiguous than their public legacy would suggest. Daniel discovers a large poster of the Isaacsons in his sister's car following her attempted suicide, a picture that explains the minor mystery of her ambiguous farewell to him in the asylum: "Goodbye, Daniel. You get the picture" (19). But the picture with its reiterated "free them," though a holy relic to Susan, is only a propaganda device to the more detached Daniel, and further ensnares rather than liberates him. Contemplating his family's public images on "this historical curio," Daniel, still a criminal of perception, has to seek out more personal recollections that can lead to more personal assessments: "I remember his cock. Face it, if I do, I do. Always shaved without clothes. She, too, shameless by design. . . everything was theory. . . . So if they walked around nude or shopped for the best meat at the lowest price, or joined the Party, it was to know the truth, to be up on it; it was the refusal to be victim; and it would justify them—their poverty, their failure, their unhappiness, and the really third-rate families they came from. They rushed after self-esteem" (41, 43).

Daniel describes his mother, Rochelle, as a realist, one who, had she not been poor, would never have been a Communist. Granting his father's genuine dedication to Marxism, Daniel nevertheless recalls his father, Paul, as being "without real resources of character" and "a selfish man" (43). And while Daniel admits that this judgment is slanted—"a moment's oversensitive perception by the little criminal of perception"—he nonetheless argues that his father had taught him "how to be a psychic alien" (45), the consequences of which affect every aspect of his life and help to explain the peculiarly unattractive streak in his character.

"Everything is Elusive"

Gradually part one ("Memorial Day") moves back toward the opening event of the central trauma: the arrest of the Isaacsons for treason. Daniel frequently juxtaposes his more recent past to the critical period of the family history in such sections as "Peekskill," in which a Paul Robeson concert leads to his father's broken arm at the hands of a rightist mob. We are introduced to the enigmatic and, to Daniel, terrifying figure of Mr. Williams, the black janitor of the Isaacsons' home and to Daniel's equally disturbing grandmother, sane and mad by turns, a token of a yet more distant and tragic family past and a prototype for Susan. And just before recalling the Peekskill sequence Daniel, trying to sum up, confesses the near impossibility of arriving at any real conclusions, an insight necessary for understanding the rest of the novel. His "mother and father . . . went to their deaths for crimes they did not commit. Or maybe they did commit them. . . . Everything is elusive. God is elusive. Revolutionary morality is elusive. Justice is elusive. Human character. Quarters for the cigarette machine" (54).

Unlike Susan, Daniel remains functional, but he also is maimed by his past and is thus a tormented, unappealing person. His sister concludes that Daniel's failure to achieve certainty concerning the truth of their past and thus the significance of the present simply indicates his own selfish weakness and a failure of revolutionary analysis. His conviction that "everything is elusive" and must necessarily remain so, however, is one of the central themes of the book and Doctorow's fiction generally, a result of the writer's imaginative integrity. Such uncertainty, emerging from the painful Isaacson life, helps make Daniel what he is.

Daniel believes that the Isaacsons' rush after self-esteem is in part based on intellectual hubris. Late in the book Daniel will toy with the idea that the novel itself is "a sequence of analyses" (296) but certainly not one analysis; moreover, Susan "died of a failure of analysis" (317)—both psychological and political—while Daniel lives on to complete his anguished vision. Nor is the reader of the novel invited to feel superior to Daniel. Among other indications, "A NOTE TO THE READER" (66) and a later direct response ("Who are you anyway? Who told you you could read this? Is nothing sacred?" [72]) suggest the necessary implication of the audience in Daniel's agonized cogitation and attempt at honesty. The second of these two direct responses reminds one of the protagonist's strategies for autobiographical honesty in *Notes from Underground,* on the one hand, and some of Barth's comic excesses in *Lost in the Funhouse* on the other. But whereas Barth's narrator may also make such a direct response, it is not always clear that the postmodernist writer really wishes to make contact with the reader, that he even believes such communication is possible. Doctorow, as we have shown through Blue's desire to touch a reader, seems quite genuinely to want the human connection, however irritating Daniel's approach might be; despite the obvious gap, Daniel's book has more in common with Dostoyevski than with Barth—especially where the elusive nature of truth is concerned.

"Everything That Came Before Is All the Same"

Book 2—"Halloween"—opens with the arrest of Selig Mindish, betrayer of the Isaacsons, and closes on the eve of their long-delayed trial. As the name implies, it is a period in which political demons, always lurking, are especially threatening in American life. The Korean War, the cold war, and nuclear terror provide the background for the red scare and the protracted indictments and preparations for the celebrated spy trial, or witch-hunt. Even before Paul is arrested, the effect on the children is acute; when first Paul and then Rochelle is taken away (after a period of either ineptitude and callousness or else psychological warfare against the family by the FBI and the justice department) Danny and Susan enter new kinds of psychological and physical prisons. For five weeks they survive the spiritually arid and loveless apartment of their father's sister Frieda, who is not so much evil as weak. Daniel, literally becoming short of breath, grows hyperactive and nearly hysterical; Susan wets the bed and starts the long metamorphosis into a starfish, a process that is postponed for years but is eventually inevitable. When their aunt can no longer function, the children are put in a grim shelter and the punitive qualities of her household become the literal conditions of their institutional life; just like their parents, they are interned by the state. Daniel's developing guilt finds an appropriate setting; as the government's case is played out in an uncritical press he starts to wonder whether his father really was a ringleader and master spy—and if so, what is he? More immediately, he comes to realize that the rapidly disintegrating Susan is now his responsibility, but that he is unable to do more than try to survive himself, partly through deception and partly through exploitation of another child, the catatonic Inertia Kid. The section ends with the children's escape from the shelter and their arduous trek across New York to their old neighborhood and home, only to find themselves locked out of the dark and shabby little house of their troubled childhood.

In this section the children's domestic and psychic trauma is brought into sharper focus; the novel's diffuse first book has given way to the exploration of a somewhat more concentrated subject matter and chronology. The emphasis on perception in the first section is necessary to prepare us for this material; in turn this material further clarifies the character of Daniel and explains much about his cruelty and strange behavior. And among the fewer but continuing interpolations of material from his later life is his thematically important meeting with the New York activist Artie Sternlicht. Sternlicht had previously discussed with Susan her plan to invest their parents' small legacy in a foundation for revolution named in their honor. Sternlicht, an Abbie Hoffman or Jerry Rubin type, is a radical's radical; his obsession with destroying the system makes possible a kind of grotesque pragmatism and totally of commitment that probably appeal to the disturbed Susan. Sternlicht and his girlfriend sing for the uncommitted Daniel the labor song "Which Side Are You On," shrieking the chorus directly in his face so that he goes home "reacquainted with the merciless radical temperament" (170). But Sternlicht also repudiates the Isaacsons and old guard American Communists for having played by establishment rules and hence having achieved nothing: "The American Communist Party set the Left back fifty years. I think they worked for the FBI" (166). Daniel hereby realizes the brutal effect that Sternlicht's indictment must have had on the unstable Susan and now understands that her enigmatic line "they're still fucking us" meant not Paul and Rochelle (as, significantly, it would have meant to Daniel) but rather "everyone else and now the Left."[4]

But still more central to the novel's concern with the elusive nature of truth and Daniel's pained attempts at cogitation (and thus the book's design) is "a collage of pictures, movie stills, posters, and real objects" (150) that covers one whole wall of Sternlicht's apartment. As a work of art it lacks any overt intention beyond an attempt to cover holes that admit the winter wind. It is unfinished and Sternlicht's girlfriend Baby, its creator, considers continuing it until it covers the whole house. It is already in the process of covering itself and new layers now hide whatever accidentally meaningful configurations it might have originally suggested. On the other hand, its very randomness, its denial of perspective, focus, and theme, its absurd and reductive juxtapositions, its radical inclusiveness (a half page of diverse items are given as examples)—all suggest a different sort of meaning. Indeed, it has a significant name: "EVERYTHING THAT CAME BEFORE IS ALL THE SAME" (151), including, presumably, the Isaacsons, whose poster should have been lodged there, from Sternlicht's point of view. A master of wit and irony, Sternlicht nevertheless fails to draw the logical conclusion; suffused with radical hubris, he casually lumps together everything that preceded his own anarchistic insight and assumes that significance starts with him. But the terrible disparateness of the wall is thematically consistent with Daniel's own conclusions and his own book has a montage, if not a collagelike quality.[5]

Doctorow has indicated in an interview with Larry McCaffery that beginning with *The Book of Daniel,* he "gave up trying to write with concern for the transition characteristic of the nineteenth-century novel," that no longer interested in realism, he deliberately employed the "idea of discontinuity" with "black-outs and running changes of voice and character," convinced that "eighty or ninety years of film technology" and the impact of television had prepared his readers (*EC,* 40–41). As Annie Dillard has pointed out, "no degree of rapid splicing could startle an audience raised on sixty second television commercials; we tend to be bored without it."[6] Doctorow's motive here is not simply novelty but rather an attempt to find a form that equates to experience, as he understands it; the narrative collage, so typical of the twentieth-century perspective, represents the nature and movement of Daniel's mind. (It is appropriate that Daniel feels that "what is most monstrous is sequence" [262].) And if Doctorow's fictional motive really were primarily didactic, as some critics argue and as he occasionally seems constrained to imply, such narrational strategy would make little sense, especially because Doctorow has on occasion claimed that he wishes to reach the largest possible popular audience. Rather, the choice corresponds to the novelist's even deeper belief that all writing is exploratory, that—when it works—it is discovery.

Family Trials

The novel's third section, "Starfish," is its most politically charged segment and the most historically located; it is here that both hostile and friendly critics (among those whose interests are more nearly thematic than aesthetic) take offense or discover merit. And on the face of it, especially isolated from the fictional and existential concerns of the other three parts, the novel does seem to offer radical analysis here.

It opens with a treatment of the emotionally heartless conditions of Paul and Rochelle's incarceration and a depiction of the trial and its major players—none of whom, ironically, are the Isaacsons. The issues appear to be more political than legal, although their own lawyer, a conservative Jew who nonetheless opposes the clear injustice inherent in politically manipulated trials, worships the rule of law. Under his tutelage, Rochelle, becoming increasingly astute and firm as Paul sinks farther into theory and despair, sums up the real issue: "Under the charge against us the normal rules of evidence are suspended. For us they don't exist. We are charged not with committing espionage, but with conspiring to commit espionage. Since espionage itself does not have to be proved, no evidence is required that we have done anything. All that is required is evidence that we intended to do something" (206). Such evidence is supplied by the earlier arrested family friend and fellow party member, Selig Mindish, whose false accusations, or betrayal, earns him a jail sentence and the Isaacsons' death. Since they are offered a chance to save their lives even after sentencing, it becomes clear that to a cynical justice system "the death sentence itself was used as an investigative procedure" (239).[7]

There is nothing in Daniel's treatment of the trial that convinces the reader that the couple is guilty of anything more criminal than their own radical analysis; indeed, narrative intimacy has quite the opposite effect.[8] Doctorow, limiting Daniel's narration here, simplifies the historical trial considerably, adapting some of its complex detail (especially the more sympathetic elements), but wisely making no attempt to deal with its murky background, labyrinthine landscape or range of participants; one can discover no new historical insights into the trial here beyond the epistemological, but discovering such is hardly Doctorow's intention. He cannot avoid the almost mythic significance of events that we now have no way definitively to assess, but his treatment is far from the "obvious paraphrase" some critics have seen it to be.[9] And if he fails to dramatize the best arguments of the prosecution, neither does he make any attempt to pursue the Rosenberg defense. Daniel, who reconstructs the story, can hardly escape his overwhelming familial involvement; his strongest materials are naturally his personal memories and imaginative reconstructions of life as a child, none of which are much help to the reader who expects insight into the historical events. And his political speculations are radically different from those of his parents and Susan. In the first place, he knows that he can only view these issues from the perspective of one whose psychological life is deeply implicated; if we can see the Isaacsons it is because we see Daniel seeing—or inventing—them. As Jerome Charyn said in his review, Daniel "mythologizes the rude details of his life."[10] Secondly, as a criminal of perception, a sort of underground man, Daniel's inevitable skepticism produces an irony missing in his fully committed relatives.

Since the Isaacsons are tried and found guilty in the press, the court's long-awaited verdict is predictable. Having been "held to account for the Soviet Union" and having been "held to account for the condition of the world today," the Isaacsons are therefore easily "convicted of conspiracy to give to the Soviet Union the secret of the atom bomb" (221). Since nothing in Daniel's reconstruction of the story supports this conclusion, the reader's interest and sympathy naturally fix on the domestic pathos. The trial and verdict are made all the more poignant by the recapitulation of the Isaacson romance, both a history of the making of two young American radicals and an account of two love stories, one personal and one ideological—romances of the Left.

After reviewing other fictional but representative and sympathetic perspectives on the trial, Daniel intrudes a highly critical analysis of the cold war itself against which the trial has taken place. This section, called "TRUE HISTORY OF THE COLD WAR: A RAGA" (248), includes a short sketch of Henry Stimson's failure to convince the Truman administration of the need for a sane foreign policy toward Russia, one that would not use the temporary American technological advantage to establish the insane nuclear arms race that ultimately resulted.[11] Appropriately enough, but without obvious comment, Book 3 returns to the present and concludes with the Pentagon march of October 1967. Daniel—surrendering his draft card and giving his name as Isaacson rather than Lewin, his adopted name—participates in the New Left's attack on rigid policies and national terrors similar to those opposed by the Old Left of the 1940s.

All of this seems to add up to what appears to be a clear political indictment, and that Doctorow largely supports a critical view of America—in both its cold war and Vietnam dimensions—is surely beyond doubt. But without in the least qualifying this personal view, the reader may still come to realize that the novelist's interest is finally not primarily in the actual innocence or guilt of the Isaacsons-Rosenbergs, nor even in social or political injustice, but rather in the ongoing synthesis of Daniel's vision. Whatever the truth or untruth of Daniel's "analysis," the main emphasis has been on the narrator-as-witness.

"Alone in the Cold War"

With the partial exception of their adoptive father, no one really understands the depth of the Isaacson children's trauma. After their parents' arrest, only Ascher, the humane family lawyer, makes any attempt to offer them emotional support. But the well-intentioned Ascher, weary, overpowered by a government bent on bringing in a guilty verdict by any means as opposed to discovering the truth, childless and ignorant of the ways of children, can help them but little. Everywhere else they meet cruelty or disregard, even from relatives. Until they become useful to the propaganda needs of the Communist party, they are more or less ignored by their parents' political friends, left "alone in the Cold War" (189). The result for Susan will be neurosis and, finally, an insanity that leads to the denial of life. In this section of the novel

Daniel describes her final withdrawal: "Today Susan is a starfish. Today she practices the silence of the starfish. There are few silences deeper than the silence of the starfish. There are not many degrees of life lower before there is no life" (223).

In the third section Daniel describes the first of the children's visits to their parents in prison. Here we can already see Susan's vulnerability; her growing instability is evident in her detachment and controlled hysteria. In a passage during which Doctorow's sympathetic imagination is at its height, Susan matter-of-factly asks her mother, "When are they going to kill you?" Controlling herself heroically, Rochelle tries to explain the legal process that stands between her and any such summary end. Susan, however, pursues the issue: "But what if they kill you anyway. . . . How will they do it?" (260–61). (Later Susan's inadvertent cruelty will extend to her father when she responds to his pathetic collection of insects by telling him "I hate it. . . . I hate dead things" [263].) Susan spends the rest of the visit tracing a dumb circuit around the visiting room walls, almost like a sleepwalker. Eventually, offered the chance for normalcy by the deeply caring Lewins, Susan will yield first to the excesses of religion and sex, then to alcohol and drugs, finally to the counterculture, whose New Left politics fill a deep and more than ideological need. But when she is betrayed by her parents' political heirs, only insanity remains as a means of escape. During that same prison visit, Daniel seems much more in control of himself than is his sister. Consciously aware of the impact their visit has on his mother, he tries to give her positive news about their life beyond the bars. And attempting to counteract the painful impact of Susan's remarks, he boasts to Rochelle that he will become a lawyer and get her free. But then his own level of understanding and emotional maturity emerges: "I won't let them kill you. . . . I'll kill them first" (261), he cries. Already he experiences something of the deep and unjustifiable guilt that will later extend to his attitude toward Susan and become so much a part of his adult life and motivation; he painfully confesses (what his mother of course knows) that while his parents languish in jail, he and his sister will live with a family in New Rochelle, that bastion of everything his parents oppose.

Thus the character and behavior of the adult Daniel—often repulsive—is prepared for. Since Daniel is the lens through which the material of this third and most political section is viewed, the juxtaposition of those childhood scenes to his comments on the trial and the cold war is critical to our understanding. That Daniel's response is anything but objective becomes clearer in momentary outbursts and in the emergence of references to electricity in this section, a topic and motif that becomes obsessive in the novel from here on until he actually describes, in painful detail in the novel's final section, the execution itself.

Therefore, when at the end of this section Daniel goes to Washington for the march on the Pentagon—"driving into the heart of darkness" (267)—it is more nearly for deeply personal reasons than for political ones that he participates as an Isaacson, not a Lewin. He has already admitted that with the up-to-date FBI file of the son of convicted spies, he is curiously insulated from the results of civil disobedience. Recalling a candlelight vigil for his condemned parents in front of the White House in which he and his sister became instant media stars, he admits that "I played Washington when I was a kid" (270). The psychological nature of the march itself is immediately signified by his awareness of "the first whispers of death by suffocation" (271), a sensation Daniel experiences in situation after situation following the separation from his parents. More important, he simply cannot escape the sense that he is an alien here, an interloper, still a criminal of perception—that his very presence has in some way "robbed the day of genius" (272). In short, he feels guilt for being among people who have a legitimate right to this demonstration, while he has "sneaked in," has not "paid," or simply does not "know something that everyone else knows" (270). Looking for some kind of satisfaction, he maneuvers himself into confrontation and is beaten bloody by the police. But there is no catharsis; even this badge of membership does not allow him to enter "the bruised cheery fellowship" (274) of other protestors. His connections are too personal and too deep, his guilt too intense; his mind is too much on his "silent Starfish girl" and he is too aware of the fact that "it is a lot easier to be a revolutionary nowadays than it used to be" (274). What might have been an act of faith with his parents, a logical fulfillment of their legacy that would clarify both the past and the present, has instead become a confused and largely existential demonstration. Whatever resolution Daniel may achieve—if any—it will not be political.

The Prophet in Disneyland

"Christmas," the short concluding section of the novel, consists primarily of Daniel's trip to California to attempt an interview with Selig Mindish, his two discussions with Mindish's daughter, Linda, and his abortive meeting with Mindish in Disneyland. The book concludes with Daniel's offer to the reader of not one but "three endings" (315). Interspersed are several flashbacks—especially the painful and long-postponed description of his parents' actual electrocution—and more cultural annotations, most signifi-

cantly the distorted but brilliant analysis of Disneyland's role in the making
and maintaining of the American consciousness.

When Daniel flies to Los Angeles, his hippie, counterculture regalia of-
fends passengers and stewardess alike and, in fact, the Isaacson Foundation
for Revolution, which he is now ostensibly promoting in Susan's absence, is
paying for this apparently antiestablishment mission. But Daniel is driven
solely by personal motives: it is his final effort to discover the truth of the
family past and hence his own identity. He now sponsors the foundation exactly because before Susan's nervous breakdown, he had repudiated it; he is
guilt-ridden. When he confronts Linda Mindish, his counterpart in another
radical family, he is able to get through her defenses only because for all the
differences between them, they share the outsider's perspective. In a passage
that produces a sort of mirror image, Daniel comes to see that Linda harbors
the same sense of the injustice of others as he does, though he had assumed
that he and his sister were the only justified victims. As dedicated to her family perspective as he is to his own and, in her own way, just as unattractive a
person as Daniel is himself (despite all her attempts to assimilate herself into
the culture that has destroyed her family), Linda holds up a mirror: "For one
moment I experienced the truth of the situation as an equitability of evil.
This is what happens to us, to the children of trials; our hearts run to cunning,
our minds are sharp as claws. Such shrewdness has to be burned into the eye's
soul, it is only formed in fire. There is no way in the world either of us would
not be willing to use our sad lives; no betrayal impossible of our pain; no use
too cheap of our patrimony" (291).

Susan, he realizes, had been destroyed by her unshakable innocence but
Linda, like Daniel, shares some terrible stain: "There was enough hard corruption in Linda Mindish and me, flawless forged criminals of perception, to
exhaust the fires of the sun" (291). Yet this insight is purely intuitive; he has
to invent Linda, as he has been forced largely to invent his parents. The
strangers he actually meets are Linda and her fiancé "Dale something"—a
couple sitting opposite him on a couch in "identical poses," a suburban version of American Gothic confronting him in icy menace. His "heart sinks in
the blank stare of their insularity and rises in rage" (288) as he realizes that his
search will be met by "nothing but deeper and deeper levels of her alienation"
(287); Linda's defense against the enemy has been to join it, just as her father
did years before. Hence she responds to Daniel with suspicion and contempt,
rejecting as absurd his "theory of the other couple" (294)—that the Isaacsons
were the scapegoats for a truly treasonous family. But enough kinship, however reluctant and negative, exists between them somehow; for whatever personal reasons—"perhaps she hated her father as well as she loved him" (301)

or simply realized that he could disclose nothing—Linda agrees to arrange a meeting between Daniel and Mindish.

That meeting takes place in the heart of Disneyland, located in "Anaheim, a town somewhere between Buchenwald and Belsen" (301), a place where the clever and efficient solutions to the problems of mass transport "would light admiration in the eyes of an SS transport officer" (306). Associations with the Holocaust are neither accidental nor gratuitous; as in the Isaacson trial itself, the principals here are still Jewish, reminding us that, in one of its dimensions, this is a Jewish novel.[12] More important, Daniel's brilliant, if outrageous, analysis of the giant theme park imputes a virtually fascist import to the great shrine of American dreams. Shaped like a womb, it is to the prophet Daniel the mechanical incubator of "mythic rituals" (302). The popular culture, which is supposed to be the healthy product of a mass democracy, has produced an amusing and apparently harmless American art form—the cartoon. But, in its Disneyland embodiment, the form suggests to the alienated Daniel sinister underlying implications. In the first place, the cartoon itself, having come "to express the collective unconsciousness of the community of the American Naïve" (303), offers a brutally reductive "theology" concerning human nature. Second, the park's five divisions—Frontierland, Tomorrowland, Fantasyland, Adventureland, and Main Street USA—work to create a reductive kitsch myth, "a sentimental compression of something that is already a lie" (304). Third, there are political implications in such reduction: "What Disneyland proposes is a technique of abbreviated shorthand culture for the masses, a mindless thrill, like an electric shock that insists at the same time on the recipient's rich psychic relation to his country's history and language and literature" (305). In short, "in this light it is possible to understand the aesthetics of cartoon adaptions as totalitarian in nature" (304). As a superior form of thought control, it provides the public with a synthetic identity, one that can be manipulated—presumably like that of the Third Reich. Robert Alter has called this sequence "monstrously disproportionate."[13] But Doctorow's "analysis" is brilliant, however maddeningly exaggerated. Moreover, and this realization is crucial, it originates in Daniel's visionary, prophetic role, not in his position as head of the Isaacson Foundation; it is an intensely located vision, one projected by a young man who by now Doctorow has portrayed as capable of insight and absurdity, kindness and sadistic cruelty. Its mock objectivity reminds us that Daniel is a "new journalist," that his subjective realizations are more important to him than cold analysis, and that history is composed.

With savage irony Doctorow has Daniel at last meet Mindish in Disney's Tomorrowland, where the old man, in whose senility the past is lost, drives one of the toy bumper cars in the Richfield Autopia. The only car owner in the Isaacson set (but a terrible driver even then), Mindish now drives "in alternating palsies of the nerve": "a moment of astonishment, a moment of pugnacity" (307). When Daniel at last is face to face with him, it is as though Mindish, too, had been electrocuted—though not killed—treated rather to a kind of massive legal shock therapy: "The whites of his eyes were discolored. . . . Brown spots and moles had attacked his skin. His white hair was thinned out. His eyes were sunken in age sockets of fat and skin. His jaw moved up and down, his lips made the sound of a faucet dripping as they met and fell apart" (308).[14] For one brief moment Mindish recognizes "Denny" and, tears in his eyes, kisses the top of the young man's head; then he is lost, again, in Tomorrowland.

Daniel's failure in this quixotic but necessary venture is followed first by a kind of encyclopedic entry on world electricity production and then by an agonized response directly to the reader: "I suppose you think I can't do the electrocution. I know there is a you. There has always been a you. YOU: I will show you that I can do the electrocution" (312). And he does, forcing himself to describe the long-delayed event in painful detail and contrasting the nearly shattered Paul with the steely Rochelle who, refusing to allow the rabbi to attend her, calls out as he leaves, "Let my son be bar mitzvahed today. Let our death be his bar mitzvah" (314). In creating this scene, Daniel is liberated.

Liberation

Daniel, having finally "done" the execution of his parents, offers three brief endings to his curious work. The first, and most oblique, describes his last visit to his old house a week after the failed California mission; a black family lives there now and when he sees them engaged in a familiar family ritual he can at last let go: "It's their house now" (315). The second ending conflates two funerals, a huge public one for the executed Isaacsons and, years later, a tiny family one for Susan, a radical innocent unable to accept reality, technically dead of pneumonia but who has actually willed herself out of life. Daniel, refusing a rabbi at the grave (as his mother had at her execution), hires itinerant Jewish prayer makers to chant the Kaddish instead and, in the midst of their paradoxically commercial and yet somehow sincere litanies, he realizes, "I think that I am going to be able to cry" (318). The third ending, "The Library," shows him having hoped to be able to "discuss some of the questions posed by this narrative" (318), being evicted from the university library by protestors instead:

"Time to leave, man, they're closing the school down."
  "Wait—"
  "No wait, man, the time is now. The water's shut off. The lights are going out.
Close the book, man, what's the matter with you, don't you know you're liberated?"
                                                                                          (318)

Some of the excesses of the counterculture are amusingly captured here, and the scene once and for all separates Daniel from those whom he only superficially resembles. But in the only way possible Daniel is liberated. ("I have to smile. It has not been unexpected" [318] is Daniel's ambiguous response.) Mindish having been faced, the executions done, the funerals described, Daniel can at last stop. Several critics have assumed these three endings to be random alternatives and cited them as evidence of the novel's failure of resolution. But the novel's three endings are not only compatible, they are actually one. The house, which Daniel and Susan had run back to earlier, had held whatever organic family life the Isaacson children would ever know; empty when they attempted to make their escape, it is filled with new life now and forever beyond his reach. The funerals end both Daniel's guilt concerning his parents and his guilt over Susan—the dead are at last buried; his tears are of compassion and relief. And the last lines of the third ending—"But thou, O Daniel, shut up the words, and seal the book, even to the time of the end. . . Go thy way Daniel: for the words are closed up and sealed till the time of the end" (319)—with their deliberate echo of the protestor's ironical command to "close the book," bring a significant measure of genuine closure to Daniel's testimony. Daniel employs multiple endings but not "multiple-choice endings," as Arthur Saltzman has called them. He admits that "analysis brings him [Daniel] into greater maturity" and that his efforts to rescue truth . . . seem directed to a more positive, redemptive purpose" than do those of Blue in *Welcome to Hard Times*. Saltzman, however, appears to regret the novel's failure to achieve some "redemptive" theme and argues that in these novels "writing itself . . . is indicted for being merely peripheral to experience" (*EC*, 87). David Gross shares Saltzman's view, pointing to Blue's "radical distrust of language itself" (*EC*, 135).

But Doctorow repeatedly asserts his skepticism, not his pessimism, about writing. Blue and Daniel have earned more of Doctorow's respect than Saltzman's argument acknowledges; however limited and provisional their achievement, both embody Doctorow's sense of the heroic in modern writing. The explanation lies in the kind of resolution that the book seeks, that, indeed, is possible. While Doctorow has called the book "an explicitly political novel," he acknowledged at the same time that he wrote the book with no conclusion in mind (*EC,* 61). In his view, virtually all novels are in some sense political, but his own at least are never didactic articulations of a preconceived social perspective—whatever his openly acknowledged convictions may be outside his fiction. As we have seen in *Welcome to Hard Times* and as several critics have shown, throughout his work Doctorow employs the theme and images of historical repetition, suggesting, at the cosmic level as well as the human, a hopeless round.[15] (Sternlicht's critique of progress and his collage entitled "everything that came before is all the same" are typical examples, but Sternlicht, like Marx, thinks that the principle of motion will end with his political deconstruction.) And at rare moments Doctorow directly admits his political pessimism: "But surely the sense we have to have now of twentieth-century political alternatives is the kind of exhaustion of them all. The only one to my mind that stands out clean and shining—because it has never really been tested in any serious way—is a philosophical position of anarchism, which at this point seems to be so totally utopian in character as not to be seriously attainable. But certainly everything else has been totally discredited: capitalism, communism, socialism. None of it seems to work" (*EC,* 65). It would be unfair, of course, to take this extraordinary statement quite literally. But surely critics who either applaud or abuse a programmatic significance in Doctorow's fiction would be well advised to recognize that starting with Blue's ruminations in *Welcome to Hard Times,* his fundamental politics are cosmic and, possibly, anarchistic.

The significance and resolution in *The Book of Daniel,* then, are almost entirely perceptual, whatever the novel's unsystematic if provocative social implications: Daniel does not exonerate his parents; he does not offer a coherent analysis of either the cold war or the counterculture; he does not provide a clear perspective for judging American society. In these regards the novel raises more questions than for which it even implies answers. It is not possible to accept, however, Estrin's view that "the completion of the work becomes, like the Ph.D. thesis it mocks, merely a meal ticket purchased towards a minimal subsistence" (*EC,* 205). In its own way the book creates a kind of order, exorcises certain ghosts, liberates Daniel from the past, allows him belatedly to assume manhood and identity. As Susan E. Lorsch points out, in Doctorow's version of the *Künstlerroman* "art does not separate the artist from his society" as is usually the case, "rather, art results from that separation and is, in fact, a healthy and valuable response to alienation."[16] At a more formal level, as Harpham puts it, "closure provides the consolation of narrative" without which neither the teller nor the audience can escape experiential chaos; "if Daniel would purchase the security of narrative, he must bring the account to closure and 'do the electrocution.' "[17]

The book's order, then, is achievable only by a criminal of perception, and the liberation it offers is the artist's victory—provisional in nature and visionary in significance. Nor do we deny the novel's moral significance in making this argument; as Doctorow has said, "Writers live in language, and their seriousness of purpose is not compromised nor their convictions threatened if they acknowledge that the subject of any given work may be a contingency of song" (*Drinks,* vi).

Chapter Four

Ragtime and the Vision of Circularity: "The World Composed and Recomposed"

The extraordinary reception and publishing history of Doctorow's *Ragtime* has been much discussed.[1] Little in the modest reception of his previous books could have prepared one to anticipate the sudden and overwhelming critical acclaim and, at the same time, widespread public enthusiasm for his fourth novel, although the warmly praised *Book of Daniel* and the very fine first novel, *Welcome to Hard Times,* had already indicated that Doctorow was a writer of some note. Perhaps because initial critical enthusiasm had been so excessive, especially in the mass media, and perhaps even more because of the sensitivity to the intense sales campaign mounted on behalf of the novel's paperback edition,[2] later critical revisions sometimes appear to debunk rather than reassess; suspecting the book of having been overrated and over-sold, critics found possible to undervalue what should have been seen, after however critical an examination, an important work.

Though the novel has not retained all of its early prestige over the decade since its publication, Doctorow's *Ragtime* still produces, even in repeated readings, the same initial sense of abundant excitement, swift movement, and dazzling artistry that produced the first flood of admiring reviews in 1975. As Bernard F. Rodgers, Jr., succinctly puts it, in *Ragtime* Doctorow has discovered "a form that is experimental and accomplished enough to appeal to critics who demand innovation and yet familiar enough to attract the common reader, and a content that grapples with the fundamental issues confronting the contemporary fictionist yet never ceases to entertain and engage."[3] Because the work continues to provoke substantial aesthetic interest as an innovative novel and because it remains thematically provocative, *Ragtime* has a secure place in contemporary American fiction.

Three Families

Ragtime is divided into three roughly equal, untitled sections, and these
are followed by a short section consisting of the fortieth chapter, which serves
as a kind of epilogue. The book's multiple narratives make paraphrase difficult, but it will be useful to remind ourselves here of the essential outline. The
novel opens with a rush of stereotypical materials drawn from the first decade
of the twentieth century—public names, references, conventional values and
assumptions—provided as a background against which to introduce the first
of the novel's three generic families, the upper middle-class characters named
simply "Father," "Mother," and "Little Boy." This family lives in a world of
sunny patriotism (Father manufactures flags and fireworks), where at first we
are told that "there were no Negroes. There were no immigrants" (4). The
sensitive Little Boy (who emerges as the novel's central intelligence) has developed an intense interest in the activities of the escape artist Harry Houdini
(only one of several historical figures mentioned in the first few pages) who,
quite by accident, intrudes upon the family's comfortable but claustrophobic
New Rochelle life one hot Sunday afternoon, the first of an ever-spreading
pattern of coincidences that the novel explores. One major device in the novel
is arranging the meetings of fictional and historical personages, as well as having historical figures meet and interact with each other fictionally.

Father, an amateur explorer both capable and affluent enough to do so,
joins Admiral Peary's expedition to the Arctic. Meanwhile, the famous trial
of the wealthy and psychotic Harry K. Thaw for the murder of architect
Stanford White opens, and Thaw's wife, the model and show girl Evelyn
Nesbit, who was the cause of the murder, becomes the passionate love ob-
ject of Mother's Younger Brother. They become lovers after Nesbit, bored
by the drawn-out trial, becomes infatuated with an accidentally discovered
but unobtainable slum child and succumbs to Younger Brother's intense, if
inept, wooing.

The child or "Little Girl" who enraptures Evelyn Nesbit is the daughter of
Tateh, a Jewish immigrant street artist and socialist, and Mameh, the wife
whom Tateh abandons after she prostitutes herself for her impoverished family. This is the book's second generic family. Just as Houdini had been previously introduced, Doctorow now brings into this group of fictional characters
the anarchist Emma Goldman who, having rescued Evelyn Nesbit from a
police raid on one of her own political rallies, gives Evelyn not only a radical
education but one of the more erotic massages in literature.

Mother discovers a newly born black child buried alive in her garden and
the child's mother, Sarah, is immediately caught. Sensing the tragedy behind

the young black woman's act as well as being moved by the child, Mother insists on taking both into her home; we thus have the beginning of the novel's third generic family. "Apparently there *were* Negroes. There *were* immigrants" (5).

While his northern adventures are eroding Father's ruling assumptions, Tateh and the Little Girl flee New York after an abortive relationship with Evelyn Nesbit. Part 1 of the novel ends as it began with Houdini as focal character desperately trying to perform acts that can compete with the events of modern life; he finds himself in Europe learning to fly a plane and meeting, by accident, Archduke Franz Ferdinand, heir to the Austro-Hungarian throne.

Part 2 opens with Father's return from the Arctic to learn of Mother's role as keeper of Sarah and her baby as well as Mother's partial liberation, sexually and socially. In Lawrence, Massachusetts, Tateh and Little Girl become embroiled in the famous mill strike of 1912 and, after being treated brutally by management goons, Tateh abandons the socialist workers' struggle. When he offered his talents to the strike, union leaders had told him "we don't want art" (140). Yet because he was an artist (he had always hated machinery), he now chooses to adopt the individualism inherent in the American experience: "Thus did the artist point his life along the lines of flow of American energy" (153). He has been rescued by the discovery that he can profitably market moving picture books; later in the novel he will appear as an early Hollywood film mogul.

More historical personages emerge as in one of the novel's most bitterly comic sections, J. P. Morgan and Henry Ford meet at Morgan's instigation to discuss Morgan's notion of their roles as continually reincarnated superhuman leaders of mankind. Immediately afterward (and already halfway through the novel) Doctorow introduces the black ragtime musician Coalhouse Walker, a genuinely superior man who has achieved success without benefit of race or wealth. Walker comes looking for Sarah and the baby that is obviously his; he returns to court Sarah to the delight of Mother. Father, a man neither evil nor so conventionally prejudiced as his peers but yet limited in his appreciation of the black race, becomes worried about Walker's role in their previously secure lives. Walker, who owns a new Ford car, is stopped on his way home from visiting Sarah by members of the Emerald Isle Fire Station, Irish immigrants who represent vicious racism and ethnic hostility. Their destruction of Walker's car becomes the source of the tragedy to follow. Father makes some attempt to help Walker, with whom he basically sympathizes, but he yields to fear and self-interest, berating Mother for having exposed the family to danger. After vainly seeking legal redress, Walker, grief-stricken by the death of Sarah (who is brutally beaten when she naively seeks help from Vice President James Sherman), destroys the Emerald Isle Fire Station, killing several of its members and promising an all-out war on New Rochelle unless his car is returned restored and the fire chief is given up to his justice. He organizes a small group of young black men to which Younger Brother, having been radicalized by Emma Goldman, will later offer himself as a bomb specialist, a trade he learned in Father's fireworks factory.

Part 3 opens with Walker's second firehouse attack and the growing public fear and anger at the gang's terrorist activities. Meanwhile, Father and Mother, achieving a partial restoration of their old relationship, take the family and their black dependent to Atlantic City for the summer. There, in an idyllic world of sun and sea, they meet Tateh, now metamorphosed into Baron Ashkenazy, film producer, and the Little Girl. The two families become quite friendly, especially the children. But beyond this island of Edenic pleasure created by wealth, class, and nature, Walker plans and carries out an occupation of J. P. Morgan's great marble library in New York, having intended to take the financier hostage and having confused the grander building with Morgan's residence. Morgan, on his way to Europe, will later cable the police to "give him his automobile and hang him" (331). When the personal intervention of Booker T. Washington fails to dissuade Walker (although it does cause him to reduce his demands to the return of his car), Father becomes a messenger, negotiator, and finally hostage. Father also confronts Younger Brother, now a full-fledged member of Walker's group, and their mutual denunciations mark the unbridgeable gap between them. After the fire chief, Willie Conklin (the craven racist responsible for the entire affair), is forced to rebuild Walker's Ford in front of the Morgan library, the police allow the little band of Walker's followers to escape in return for his surrender; Father remains behind to guarantee that both sides honor their agreement.

In the book's short concluding section Walker surrenders, stepping out of the library into a hail of bullets brought on either by the authorities' interpretation of Morgan's command or else by some gesture of Walker's intended to achieve the same effect. Having inherited the car, Younger Brother successfully escapes ever farther south, eventually ending up amidst the Mexican Revolution where, fighting for Zapata, he finally is killed. Morgan travels to Egypt to experience directly the function of the pyramids in reincarnation and plans to build his own pyramid there. A night spent alone in the king's chamber of the Great Pyramid turns into a fiasco and, catching cold, Morgan begins a fatal decline; his faith in his own reincarnation as one of the world's chosen leaders, however, remains unshaken.

The novel moves to its close as the First World War approaches—"the signs of the coming conflagration were everywhere" (355). Houdini learns of the assassination of Archduke Ferdinand and, returning us to the book's first chapter, he recalls as his only "mystical experience" (366) the Little Boy's then cryptic command to "warn the Duke" (11).

With Sarah and Walker dead, Mother retains their black child, but her marriage is reduced to a mere formality. Father sails on the *Lusitania* and is lost when the ship is sunk by a German U-boat; he had been on his way to England to deliver some of the tools of war that Younger Brother had invented before his defection to the Walker revolt. Mother and Tateh-Baron Ashkenazy, having been mutually attracted to each other at Atlantic City, now marry and move to California; with the Little Boy, the Little Girl, and the black child they ironically compose a microcosm of the melting pot always promised but, as the novel argues, never achieved by that innocent America now forever lost.

Narrative Range

This brief paraphrase can only hint at the essential qualities of the novel, for example its extensive narrative range. We have not mentioned the narrator's running commentary on the social and political life of America—among other things, the roles and terms of presidents Teddy Roosevelt, William Howard Taft, and Woodrow Wilson are discussed—nor how in Doctorow's view these fundamental elements of "our history" were affected by American technology and economics. Henry Ford is important to the novel's plot in his relationship with J. P. Morgan but, more important, he is central to those social themes the nexus of which is the relationship between capitalism and technology. Beyond this issue lies the less obvious but thematically more important function he serves in the theme of circularity and repetition, to which we will later return.

The novel's range is extended in a number of similar ways. There is, for instance, the amusing sequence detailing the visit to America by Freud and Jung; among other clever touches, Doctorow has the two famous psychological pioneers ride through the tunnel of love together at Coney Island and Freud cuts short his visit to America because of the shortage of public toilets. But this witty sequence has much more than comic value; along with other figures, Freud and Jung represent the emerging intellectual complexity of modern life, especially as it impinges upon the mythic innocence of the "new world." Freud is convinced that "America is a mistake, a gigantic mistake" (44), while to the American public Freud "appeared as some kind of German sexologist, an exponent of free love who used big words to talk about dirty things" (39). He is denied in America for a decade or more but "would have his revenge and see his ideas begin to destroy sex in America forever" (39). Freud connects the book's social critique with the modern intellectual explosion and, in the logic of Doctorow's method of juxtaposition, provides other relevant connections. He is introduced, for example, immediately after a reference to Houdini, "a Jew [who] . . . was passionately in love with his ancient mother. . . . the last of the great shameless mother lovers" (39).

In such a complex we must also locate Evelyn Nesbit and Emma Goldman, linked both by mysterious spiritual "correspondences" (68) and by common social realities; both are associated with the nascent feminist movement and both suggest wider implications as well. Nesbit is presented as "the first sex goddess in American history" (95), a product of capitalism (the popular culture of which is so closely related to that economic system) and of the nature of American sexuality, itself deeply influenced by economics and long-established sexual politics. Goldman, who actually does advocate free love and is the novel's major source of both sexual and political idealism, is herself an immigrant (at the novel's end she is deported), and her relationship with Nesbit is crucial, not only to the plot but to its ever-widening set of references to American values. Linking sex and politics, she is also connected to Nesbit's lover, Younger Brother, for the latter is as much influenced by his own sexual anxieties and repressed longings as he is by Goldman's "bracing linguistics of radical idealism" (58), which impress even Nesbit. Thus, the much debated scene in which Goldman massages Nesbit and Younger Brother watches from the closet is far from simple voyeurism, a charge that has been leveled. Its cresendo—an extraordinary tour de force even if taken out of context—occurs when the enormously aroused young man, "his face twisted in a paroxysm of saintly mortification," falls headlong out of Goldman's closet where he had been watching (like Satan spying on Milton's Eve or Porphyro peeking at Keats's Madeline): "He was clutching in his hands, as if trying to choke it, a rampant penis which, scornful of his intentions, whipped him about the floor, launching to his cries of ecstasy or despair, great filamented spurts of jism that traced the air like bullets and then settled slowly over Evelyn in her bed like falling ticker tape." (71)

Responding to this scene in *Moral Fiction,* the novelist John Gardner quotes Tolstoy on de Maupassant in order to prove the absence of "a correct moral relation" to what is portrayed here, accusing Doctorow of describing "certain obscenities difficult to understand." Then sniffing at the "fraudulence" and "chicanery," Gardner absurdly comments that "things do not happen in the world as Doctorow claims they do. Even in the hands of young and highly excited men, penises do not behave as Doctorow maintains."[4] But even the mythic mode of the novel need not be cited to account for this passage (which, Gardner not withstanding, is only an exaggeration not a falsification); sexually, psychologically, and even culturally the imagery is wonderfully evocative.

"Do Not Play This Piece Fast"

Many other topics are also explored—for instance, public taste, fads, sports and the arts—in what might be loosely called the novel's encyclopedic design, a design typical of satire. And critical to our experience of this broad range of materials is the pace at which they are presented (a pace dictated by the novel's attitude toward these materials but also by their very number and variety), and the style with which they are related. As his only epigraph Doctorow quotes this appeal from Scott Joplin, the most famous of ragtime composers: "Do not play this piece fast. It is never right to play Ragtime fast." We may take this as significant authorial warning, yet it is actually difficult to read the novel slowly and methodically; Doctorow also said that he had wanted "to write something that was absolutely relentless," full of energy.[5] In the first place, the encyclopedic materials here cited are presented in a series of forty swiftly delivered, short chapters averaging less than ten pages each. Moreover, despite the real complexity of his topic, Doctorow employs the deceptive simplicity of storybook narration. We are not, initially, invited to pause anywhere and look closely at anything.

In addition to Doctorow's rhetoric, this cumulative effect is achieved by rejecting an overarching linear plot line in favor of the cleverly collated stories of his three generic families and the historical figures with whom they often interact. Cinematically constructed out of a series of scenes, situations, and interwoven stories, the plot is protean and constantly shifting, denying the reader the comfort of any continuous line of development, although it generally moves ahead in time.[6] Nor do the public events provide a clear cause and effect continuity. Though it starts in 1902 and concludes with World War I, the effect is not one of historical chronicle but rather of context—a sort of collage of people and events located roughly in the ragtime era.

The novel's style firmly reinforces this sense of rapidity. Sentences, like chapters, are usually short (though offset by long paragraphs), rhetorically simple and inevitably declarative, thus achieving a kind of staccato effect; many reviewers have seen a kind of prose version of ragtime music in

Doctorow's style. The gulf between the prose of *Ragtime* and that of *The Book of Daniel* is enormous; rarely overtly thoughtful or meditative, the simplicity of style here encourages speed.[7]

Commenting on this simplicity, Doris Grumbach has noted that the hasty reader may mistakenly conclude "that a kind of surface Dick-and-Jane-and-Spot prose has been utilized to increase the reader's sense of the childlike atmosphere of the time."[8] But while the tone can at moments achieve lyrical simplicity, it is typically characterized by an irony ranging from the innocently bland to the bitterly comic, and this irony significantly qualifies the usual effect of such stylistic simplicity.

Ragging Time

Together with the narrative range, tempo, and simple prose style of *Ragtime,* the novel's largely ironic tone creates the sort of comically flattened surface associated with newsreels, cartoon strips and the silhouette—all media forms relative to the novel's subject matter and themes. This quality has delighted many readers and irritated others, depending on how they respond to the impersonal narrative voice or the satire that lies behind and produces these effects. Although, as we will see, the narrator ultimately turns out to be, or is located near, the Little Boy, the narrative voice is cool, aloof, detached. The comedy resulting from Doctorow's satire of imagined innocence and brutal cultural realities partakes of the same qualities; it lacks the warmth and the positive element inherent in traditional comedy. In a typical passage, Doctorow speaks of the exploitation of adult workers and then adds: "Children suffered no discriminatory treatment. They were valued everywhere they were employed. They did not complain as adults tended to do. . . . If there was a problem about employing children it had to do only with their endurance. They were more agile than adults but they tended in the latter hours of the day to lose a degree of efficiency. . . . They had to be counseled to stay alert. . . . One hundred children [a year] were mutilated. There seemed to be quotas for these things" (45–46). Elsewhere, speaking of Father's reflections on Coalhouse Walker's tact and bearing, the narrator says that "it occurred to Father . . . that Coalhouse . . . didn't know he was a Negro. . . . He seemed to be able to transform the customary deferences practiced by his race so that they reflected to his own dignity rather than the recipient's" (185–86). These are easily identified examples of overt critical irony, but much of the prose remains more enigmatic and elusive, only hinting at its amused or sardonic attitude—or else, like a time bomb, revealing its ironic intent only after some reflection on the reader's part.

To achieve the effect he desired, Doctorow claims to have chosen a narrative "voice that was mock historical-pedantic."[9] It is not always easy to come to terms with this peculiar tone, for the recognition of Doctorow's satiric irony is not the whole issue; the tone is made still more complex by the inclusion of a mythic element that also profoundly determines our reaction.

History as Myth

There are, in fact, other qualities more important than narrative range, tempo, and tone. A simple plot summary may seem to locate Doctorow's focus at the traditional center of the novel, in plot and character, but clearly his interest lies elsewhere. If readers' root experience with *The Book of Daniel* is perhaps an unwilling but deep sympathy with the protagonist's existential pain, their fundamental reaction to *Ragtime* may be to acknowledge, perhaps in some instances also unwillingly, the sheer cleverness of the novel's execution, a realization largely unassociated with an empathetic response to the novel's characters, even those who, like the black musician Coalhouse Walker, share something of Daniel's suffering. Readers may, in fact, feel that the intelligence at the novel's center is remote and cruel, that it wields a wit as cold and sharp as a razor—but acknowledge that intelligence they must.

Because of the peculiarly distanced and seemingly aloof narrative voice here (so very different from such fully engaged Doctorow narrators as Blue), because of the archetypal nature of characterization, and because of the speed and cinematic nature of the narrative line, readers must be especially alert to the kind of novelistic experience Doctorow creates. Here, as in each of his previous and subsequent books, the novelist has shifted ground and attempted a different fictional mode, one more nearly unique than any other that he had attempted to date. *Welcome to Hard Times* and *Big as Life* exploit popular genres—the western and science fiction respectively—and *Daniel* can be classed as a sort of counterculture bildungsroman. But *Ragtime,* in both its treatment of people and history and its execution, is a much more difficult book to define.

This difficulty results, in the first place, from Doctorow's attempt in *Ragtime* to undertake an extraordinary mythic history of the first fifteen years of this century. He appears, in fact, to be an author obsessed with "History, that pig, biting into the heart's secrets" (*Daniel,* 115). Each of Doctorow's novels involves, in one way or another, a recreation of the past. In *Ragtime,* however, Doctorow has, so far, most obviously joined his contemporaries—one thinks especially of Robert Coover—who have denied the past its objective value while at the same time they have insisted upon its mythic significance.

Doctorow has said that "certain details were so delicious that I was scrupulous about getting them right. Others demanded to be changed, people's lives demanded to be mythologized." He also claims to be no longer sure which historical "facts" he invented and which he took from recorded history.[10] In fact, his book literally "defies facts;" it is "a novelist's revenge" against the sadly diminished story-telling role to which the novelist has been reduced by other forces in the culture (for example, social scientists and television), which have appropriated traditional narrative materials and relegated the novelist to the "realm of personal experience."[11]

This attitude, however undercut by practice, suggests Doctorow's sympathies with European fiction. While the "realm of personal experience" has always been the chosen ground of American literature since the Puritans first began to explore the drama of the individual soul, Doctorow, at least in theory, demands that the novelist accept an overt social responsibility. Elsewhere he blames not outside forces but American novelists themselves for a willingness "to dwell in a sort of unresounding private life." Since "the future for any of us is not individual," he advocates "books with less polish and self-consciousness, but ones about the way power works in our society, who has it, and how it is making history."[12] Considering on one side the enormous polish (and one could argue self-consciousness) of *Ragtime,* and on the other the way the novel explores power and the roots of modern history, we come to understand something of Doctorow's complexity as a novelist.[13]

He casually described his historical method in *Ragtime* this way: "I looked at pictures, I read biographies, I used what caught my attention. It's a peculiar process."[14] Such an admission may sound ominous to one concerned with history as a discipline, yet in this context the "peculiar process" is not in the least mysterious; it is the artist at work inventing reality. What intrigues us about his portrait of J. P. Morgan, for instance, is wholly imagined, not recorded; the documented past is not at issue.

In one sense, of course, the argument that has been raised by the practice of fictionalizing history—and there are those with strong reservations as to the legitimacy of such distortion—is but a logical extension of the ancient one concerning the superiority of the probable impossibility to the improbable possibility; the ultimate issue remains truth, though the nature of that truth and the means for arriving at it are subject to debate. We should be reluctant to deny the artist any use of "reality." Given widespread historical illiteracy, however, it is possible to understand why some readers argue that in such cases as *Ragtime,* distortion of recorded fact may play havoc with public knowledge. Ours is a culture that is at once antihistorical and yet, at the same time, one that seems to place a touching faith in any apparent factualness—a paradox that allows simultaneously for the devaluation of literature as a source of truth and for the insistence on "realism" as a literary value and the popular historical novel as a privileged fictional mode. This paradox in part explains the great commercial success of popular historical novelists such as James Michener and Louis L'Amour.

The serious mythologizing novelist who moves into this knowledge vacuum must establish his own priorities, must decide in favor of historical consensus or imaginative reinterpretation. Like such writers as John Barth in *The Sotweed Factor* and Thomas Pynchon in *Gravity's Rainbow,* Doctorow has in *Ragtime* chosen to write what Robert Scholes terms "fabulation," an antirealistic fictional mode that when its content is historical, produces works that "deliberately challenge the notion that history may be retrieved by objective investigation of fact."[15] Scholes finds a line in Robert Coover's novel *The Public Burning* to be a key to historical fabulation: "What if we broke all the rules, played games with the evidence, manipulated language itself, made History a partisan ally?"[16] Since Coover's speaker is Richard Nixon, the sentiment is cynically appropriate, but the approach extends more generally to books like *Ragtime,* which do just these things. Doctorow has argued that "facts are the images of history, just as images are the data of fiction" and that "as a novelist" he "could claim that history is a kind of fiction . . . and fiction is a kind of speculative history" (*EC,* 24–25). He has, in fact, flatly asserted that "there is no true fiction or nonfiction. . . . there is only narrative" (*EC,* 26). This is true because "all history is composed," thus "when you write about imaginary events in the lives of undisguised people, you are proposing that history has ended and mythology has begun" (*EC,* 43).

Whatever their factual base, then, Doctorow's historical characters are primarily interpretations, not historical recapitulations: J. P. Morgan is an idea, the creative drive of capitalism atrophied into selfish and absurd eccentricity; Henry Ford is one of Faulkner's Snopes clan come north, the ruthless force of a single mechanical idea; Emma Goldman is the embodiment of sexual and political idealism; Harry Houdini represents the dilemma of the modern artist. *Ragtime* is history composed as music, and these characters are the instruments on which some of its themes are played.

Beyond Allegorical Implications

In *Ragtime* "the characters are figures rather than people," Roger Sale ad-
miringly says, and "the result is all surface, but the surface shimmers and
shines."[17] Attacks on the novel by those who do not share Sale's enthusiasm
for Doctorow's shimmering surface, when they are not simply the result of
differing political views, in many cases suggest the still potent if submerged
struggle between readers who insist on "realism" as an index of literary value
or historical treatment and those "anti-realist" critics (largely conditioned first
by classic modernism and then by the postmodernist evolution) who are
committed to more metaphorical uses of fiction. Doctorow's use of stereo-
types (such as Father, Mother, Tateh) is a sufficient indication of his representative intention here; his characters indeed are "figures" with social, not
psychological, value. However we react to these characters, we are not required to treat them as realistic human studies and we are, in fact, largely denied the usual empathetic possibilities. In other words, just as his historical
figures are metaphorical and symbolic rather than realistic, so the largely
nameless invented characters are clearly just as much reference points as they
are particularized reality.

In Doctorow's scheme, for example, Father portrays the privilege and in-
effectuality of the WASP; Coalhouse Walker embodies the natural aristoc-
racy of the black; Tateh dramatizes the creative energy of the immigrant.
Immediately after it was published, some reviewers recognized this quality in
Ragtime. Joseph Moses, for instance, claimed that Doctorow's characters "are
allegories of American history, of the melting pot, of the making good in
technological, democratic U.S.A. Whatever the intricacies of their roles, they
follow prescribed allegorical destinies as surely as characters in Hawthorne."[18]
Moses is certainly right, both in his description of the allegorical nature of
characterization and in his conviction that Doctorow's political convictions
determine much of his allegory. But we must note this important qualifica-
tion: these characters act out their roles as fictional counters in an ambiguous
fable that may have as much in common with some elements of Kafka's obscure allegories as it does with the morally predictable world of a lot of truly
didactic fiction. It is the case here again, as in *Daniel,* that despite Doctorow's
firm political convictions, his artistic perception exceeds or escapes—or actually subverts—the control of straightforward thematic intention.

While Freud is preoccupied with the indignities of American urban life,
Karl Jung, seeing the Little Girl in a slum street, feels a "shock of recognition,
although at the moment he could not have explained why" (43). This is exactly the reader's experience at various points in the novel; and the question

arises as to whether that sense of recognition, of implied meaning, of an almost mystical sense of connection, comes from real substance or from Doctorow's Houdini-like sleight-of-hand tricks. Reading the novel, we gradually discover a network of such connections, of almost Baudelaire-like correspondences, but may it not be that Doctorow suggests more than exists, that all that seems pregnant with elusive meaning is certainly not profound but rather the result of his skill as opposed to his insight?

Doctorow is never more concerned with surface than he is in *Ragtime,* and his fascination with Houdini certainly offers us a clue to that preoccupation. Yet dazzling literary "trickery" notwithstanding, these moments of implied significance (sometimes the reverse of Wordsworth's time spots in that they predict the future, rather than invoke the past) do suggest a fundamentally deeper experience in this novel than that produced either by clever technique or social criticism. What we come to perceive is the profound evocativeness of apparently disparate experience—the endless repetition in different spheres where everything keeps happening—which dramatizes the novel's central theme. Located beyond, or even in conflict with, his more accessible political views lies the dark principle that all motion is circular, not linear, a subject to which we will return at the end of this chapter.

"Political Romance"

Sale points out that in *Ragtime* Doctorow's "impudence is both witty and grave" and, he argues, "treat it as game and it will turn serious; treat it as serious and it becomes fun."[19] This is an important point, emphasizing the ambivalence that produces ambiguity in all of Doctorow's work but especially in *Ragtime.* From Martin Green's point of view this duality is problematical; he sees it as a conflict between "playful and ironic and sophisticated . . . nostalgia" on one hand and a "radical severity of [political] judgment" on the other, which produces false characters—for instance a romanticized Coalhouse, Mother, and Tateh and an unfairly abused Father.[20] He feels that Doctorow's problem is to be caught between the playful and elegant artistic inclinations of a Vladimir Nabokov and his own more serious political inclinations. We know that in *Ragtime* Doctorow had hoped to achieve a "high seriousness" that could be made accessible to a very large audience of people who work in factories and garages (a claim labeled arrogant and condescending by some). But at the same time, his most "undemocratic" sympathies with experimental fiction and his purely existential attraction to the truth of the private imagination—despite his warning against it—emerge in *Daniel* and flourish here in *Ragtime*.

The indictment is far stronger in Greil Marcus, who finds that *Ragtime* is uncomfortably like the popular contemporary film *Nashville*. He sees Albert Murray's judgment in *Omni-Americans* as relevant here: "What most American fiction seems to represent these days is not so much the writer's actual sense of life as some theory of life to which he is giving functional allegiance."[21] Marcus believes that the result in *Ragtime* is a totally dishonest and empty novel: "Once you have read the book, there is absolutely nothing more to be gotten from it. It is dead on the page; it implies nothing, suggests nothing, never makes you stop and think, never makes you puzzle out motives, because there really are none."[22] Obviously this does not describe the reaction of most readers. Marcus's view clearly demands, among other things, that we accept certain assumptions concerning fiction's true province (which appears to be "the writer's actual sense of life,"[23] whatever that is). Such an argument must be questioned both on theoretical and practical grounds, but Marcus, along with other hostile critics, nonetheless helps us to define the kind of fiction found in *Ragtime*.

Marcus's indictment of *Ragtime* for a dishonesty resulting from reliance on theory rather than on life and the novel's doubleness as seen by Sale and Green, are reinforced in a one-sided review by Hilton Kramer, entitled "Political Romance." Kramer, seemingly angry that Doctorow's novel can offer a "delectable aesthetic surface" while at the same time anatomizing American middle-class culture—that Doctorow "can have it both ways"[24]—applies Richard Chase's seminal distinction between the novel and the romance to repudiate *Ragtime*. Reminding us that Chase equates the novel with realism, he quotes a passage from Chase that echoes one of Marcus's own assumptions: as a form, "the novel renders reality closely and in comprehensive detail." Romance on the other hand—and thus *Ragtime*—produces a work in which character is likely to be "abstract and ideal" and the "astonishing events" of the plot "are likely to have a symbolic or ideological, rather than a realistic, plausibility."[25] Kramer never acknowledges that Chase has no bias in favor of the novel over the romance (or, indeed, that he sees the romance as a fundamentally American fictional form), and Kramer actually seems to imply that Doctorow's dishonesty lies exactly in his willingness to mythologize rather than to portray realistically. That Kramer is as much repelled by the politics of Doctorow's romance as he is by the mode itself is also fairly obvious.[26] Yet, paradoxically, Kramer identifies, even if he repudiates, one of the novel's basic qualities. "According to Doctorow himself," Paul Levine notes, "he is writing in the same romance tradition as Hawthorne."[27]

Myth as History

Sale, Marcus, and Kramer, each, in differing ways, either denies or distorts the metaphorical life of *Ragtime*. Yet, as we have earlier argued, it is this very fablelike, mythic quality that gives the novel its distinctive character and that readers must recognize if they are not to mistakenly judge it in expectation of other literary qualities, especially those of historical realism. Kramer is therefore correct in identifying *Ragtime* with romance, however he misjudges Doctorow's use of that mode.

The sense of mythic dimension emerges again and again in the work—in language, character, situation and general ambience. Here is an obvious example:

Back home a momentous change was coming over the United States. There was a new President, William Howard Taft, and he took office weighing three hundred and thirty-two pounds. All over the country men began to look at themselves. They were used to drinking great quantities of beer. They customarily devoured loaves of bread and ate prodigiously of the sausage meats of poured offal that lay on the lunch counters of the saloons. The august Pierpont Morgan would routinely consume seven-and eight-course dinners. He ate breakfasts of steaks and chops, eggs, pancakes, broiled fish, rolls and butter, fresh fruit and cream. The consumption of food was a sacrament of success. A man who carried a great stomach before him was thought to be in his prime. Women went into hospitals to die of burst bladders, collapsed lungs, overtaxed hearts and meningitis of the spine. There was a heavy traffic to the spas and sulphur springs, where the purgative was valued as an inducement to the appetite. America was a great farting country. All this began to change when Taft moved into the White House. His accession to the one mythic office in the American imagination weighed everyone down. His great figure immediately expressed the apotheosis of that style of man. Thereafter fashion would go the other way and only poor people would be stout. (93–94)

We have quoted at length from this representative passage because it so fully illustrates Doctorow's approach in *Ragtime*. Here, as is so often the case in the novel, reality is in the process of slipping into pure myth. Our understanding, or more accurately, our impression of American life in this period, is forced toward imaginative generalization and oversimplification. Size, while remaining critically ironic, takes on heroic proportions in American life before the arrival of the truly huge President Taft forces a revision. Experience becomes generic, categorical, pushed to the extreme, and American taste emerges in silhouette. This can be seen in the deadly humor of the conclusion: after Taft, only poor people would be fat. The satirical element is present but restrained enough so that the humor is, at the moment of experience but probably not later, untroubling.

Other qualities that we have previously mentioned are also in evidence: the rapid pace of short, staccato sentences (of fourteen in the paragraph, ten are brief) suggests Doctorow's typical style. Taft and Morgan lose any connection with conventional reality, illustrating Doctorow's usual treatment of historical figures. The passage, like the novel as a whole, shows the novelist abandoning realistic portrayal for fabulation. As Thomas Evans has perceptively noted, for Doctorow, "the key to understanding history lies in the recurrent images of popular culture," like those above; "even the most rudimentary narrative may take on mythopoeic overtones." In *Ragtime* he "deliberately confounds factual and fictive detail in such a way that facts become ultimately less important than the metaphors that Doctorow believes illuminate the development of twentieth-century civilization."[28]

To Warn the Duke: Narrative Strategy

We have already mentioned the enigmatic, aloof quality of the novel's narrative voice. Technically third person, the perspective is clearly omniscient. Yet simultaneously the narrator has something familiar about him, too, some sense of intimacy that seems to contradict the official distance. In the first place, the narrator's frequent "we" is specifically enough located to implicate an American audience in the events of its own culture and past. Beyond that, there is something of the sense of an elderly acquaintance reminiscing; he dates his story "today, nearly fifty years" since Houdini's death (8).

Examined more closely, however, we realize that the narrator's knowledge seems most closely to approximate that which might have accrued to the Little Boy, had he chosen, as a middle-aged man, to look back. Indeed, among the numerous clues to support such an assumption, Doctorow plants two key events. The first comes only a few pages into the novel when the Little Boy, having been strangely alert to the unexpected arrival of Houdini (just before he appears the boy grows "suddenly restless"), offers the famous escape artist three words of advice: "Warn the Duke" (11). Inexplicably dropped in at the end of the first chapter, these words can easily be missed or forgotten in the rapidly accelerating and broadening novel. Alert readers, however, will be urged to return to that passage when, at the very end of the novel, Houdini himself recalls the image that had accompanied these words, an image "of a small boy looking at himself in the shiny brass headlamp of an automobile" (365). It is now 1914 and Houdini, dangling upside down in a straightjacket from a tall building in one of his incessant escape stunts, suddenly thinks of the lately assassinated Archduke Franz Ferdinand whom he had once briefly met. The abrupt linkage of the boy's warning and image in the headlight and the duke's death creates a moment of recognition that Houdini considers "the one genuine mystical experience of his life" (366).

The Little Boy is an attractive candidate for the role of narrator, and there is abundant evidence to support the idea that he plays this role. "He saw through things," we are told, "and noted the colors people produced and was never surprised by a coincidence" (305). Especially in chapter 15, Doctorow develops him as an artist figure (one of four in the novel, the other three being Houdini, Tateh and, to a lesser extent, Walker). Here we learn that he "lived an entirely secret intellectual life," that he "treasured anything discarded," since in his mind "the meaning of something was perceived through its neglect." Moreover, "he was alert not only to discarded materials but to unexpected events and coincidences" (131)—a fairly precise description of Doctorow's overall approach to the narrative of *Ragtime*. Above all, he has the modern artist's vision of life in which "nothing was immune to the principle of volatility, not even language" (133); hence it becomes "evident to him that the world composed and recomposed itself constantly in an endless process of dissatisfaction" (135)—perhaps the clearest statement of Doctorow's underlying theme of circularity, which dominates this book and appears frequently in his other books.

As narrator, moreover, the Little Boy has a rich and complex source of information and intuition. The latter includes his response to stories from Ovid, photographs, moving pictures, phonograph records—even the images made by skaters on the ice and his own reflection in the mirror.[29] The narrator cites direct sources of information as well, most of them associated with the Little Boy's life: Father's letters from Greenland and his Arctic journals, Younger Brother's silhouettes and diaries from Harlem to Mexico, newspaper clippings, Walker's letters to officials, Houdini's private, unpublished papers, and the family archives.[30]

Looked at this way, the sudden shift from third to first person at the novel's end—"Poor Father, I see his final exploration" (368)—confirms the identity of the narrator. If for obvious technical reasons the Little Boy cannot be *Ragtime*'s narrator literally—point of view here embraces a breadth of knowledge that stretches from minute particularity to the cosmic—he can, however, be seen, as Anthony Dawson aptly suggests, as "the privileged consciousness of the novel, the organizing mind of its vision."[31] It is not, in other

words, in the simple chronology of a realistic story that we must locate the
narrator; Doctorow intends no conventional mystery of hidden identity. The
boy obviously knows something that in reality he cannot, but in the dislocation of time, perception, and knowledge "realistic" fictional values are rejected in favor of an act of imagination. In Constance Pierce's words, "the
visionary child is obviously a fabrication and therefore a violation of the history the narrator/writer purports to depict in the novel."[32] This denial of conventional sequence is, as we have seen, the literary method of *The Book of
Daniel,* and in Doctorow's next novel, *Loon Lake,* the narrator will apologize
"for rendering nonlinear thinking in linear language" (*Loon,* 158), for being
unable to avoid the "helpless linear translation of the unending love of our simultaneous but disynchrous lives" (*Loon,* 300). Despite Doctorow's pro-
claimed desire for a vast, unliterary audience for *Ragtime,* then, as an artist he
clearly assumes at the same time some readership sufficiently schooled in
postmodernism to recognize the dislocation of traditional fiction by elements
of self-reflexivity, a tendency already inherent even in the apparently straightforward materials and manner of *Welcome to Hard Times.*

As we have noted, the Little Boy, while the most important, is not the only
artist figure in *Ragtime* and, to differing degrees, the novel assumes shape
and theme as a result of three others. Tateh, the socialist immigrant from Latvia, initially makes his living as a silhouette artist on the street before his metamorphosis into Baron Ashkenazy, the new genius of American film: "With
his scissors he suggested not merely outlines but textures, moods, character,
despair" (51), we are told, and this description also fits Doctorow's method
and achievement in the novel. "Silhouettes depend on the relationship between background and foreground in special dimensions," Susan Brienza reminds us, "in temporal and aural dimensions it might be said that ragtime
also depends on this relationship between background and foreground. In
short, ragtime appears to be a musical version of the moving silhouettes."[33]
This fusion of visual and aural forms becomes clear in the narrator's description of Walker's Scott Joplin recital for the family: "This was a most robust
composition, a vigorous music that roused the senses and never stood still a
moment. The boy perceived it as light touching various places in space, accu-
mulating in intricate patterns until the entire room was made to glow with its
own being" (183–84).

The performer of this music, ragtime musician Walker, also embodies artistic significance, though of a more sociological nature. It is obvious that the
status of the popular artist generally and more specifically in racial (or, in
Houdini's case, ethnic) terms is ambiguous; in great demand by a wide spectrum of the public—this is the age in which the popular culture starts to

achieve its hegemony over high culture, as the rapid growth of the moving-picture industry demonstrates—both Walker and Houdini are nonetheless undervalued or held in contempt by more influential elements of society. Father, after hearing the "intricate patterns" of Walker's ragtime, asks for "coon songs" (184); Houdini is booked by the wealthy society hostess Mrs. Stuyvesant Fish to accompany a freak show.

Exerting a very different kind of influence on the novel is the magician-escape artist Harry Houdini. While the Little Boy embodies the profound insight of the imagination and Tateh's silhouettes suggest a kind of stylized mimesis, Houdini offers us an image of the artist-as-illusionist, a dramatization of the relationship between the modern artist and his society. The Little Boy, as Doctorow's sixth novel *World's Fair* seems to confirm, may embody some spiritual autobiography; and Doctorow has indicated a personal empathy with the character of Tateh. Yet from an artistic point of view, Doctorow may more closely identify with Houdini than with the others. On the face of it, such an argument might seem strange. Houdini, emotionally tied to his mother, remains in some sense an adolescent. Though a Jew, a child of immigrants, and a witness to the outrages of vast wealth, Houdini "never developed what we think of as a political consciousness. He could not reason from his own hurt feelings" (38).

But in fundamental ways Houdini dramatizes those artistic concerns that transcend Doctorow's political and social perspective. Though his fame grows greater performance by performance, Houdini's satisfaction with his work continually shrinks. This paradox reminds us that he is, in some sense, Doctorow's Hunger Artist. Houdini's frustration with his audience and his decision to undertake a European tour—"In some peculiar way, he still felt, the people in Europe understood him better than his own countrymen" (113)—suggest strong parallels with Kafka's famous story. He is the creator never satisfied with his own creative achievement, the writer always aware of the gap between the enormity of experience in all its often ineffable forms and the finished story. And as though responding to novelist Phillip Roth's well-known observation concerning the ever-widening gap between the actual but increasingly extraordinary and incomprehensible modern life and the struggling writer's attempt to portray it, Houdini precisely articulates the dilemma: "There was a kind of act that used the real world for its stage. He couldn't touch it. For all his achievements he was a trickster, an illusionist, a mere magician. What was the sense of his life if people walked out of the theatre and forgot him? The headlines on the newsstand said Peary had reached the Pole. The real-world act was what got into the history books" (112).

Houdini's concern represents Doctorow's own sense of the gap between ever-elusive meaning and his own interpretation, and may partially account for his preempting of history. In a metaphorically relevant but seemingly unrelated early passage in the novel Doctorow shows the novelist Theodore Dreiser, the great naturalist whose fiction was intended to capture reality, endlessly and unsuccessfully turning "his chair in circles seeking the proper alignment" (30) through the night, another instance of the Little Boy's realization of the "endless process of dissatisfaction." Though a very different kind of novelist—Doctorow firmly rejects Dreiser's realism—he, too, understands the artist's compulsion to seek and inability to find the precise angle of vision, as Daniel's narrative so clearly reveals. And Doctorow, having chosen stylistic and technical complexities that repudiate realism, appreciates the limitations felt by Houdini the illusionist, how "the real-world" act takes supremacy in the "history books" (112). It is just such supremacy that Doctorow's own mythic history seeks to defeat. Despite his differences from the great escape artist, then—for Doctorow certainly has a well-developed "political consciousness"—Houdini is central to our understanding of the novel at its deepest thematic level. It is significant that it is Houdini who most fascinates and impresses the Little Boy who is the narrative center of the book.

These artist figures, then, help illuminate the point of view, the general mode, and some dimensions of the novel's themes. And the endless silhouettes that Tateh cuts of the Little Girl, the repetitive escape stunts performed with ever more desperate intensity by Houdini, and every sort of "duplicated event" (133) that intrigues the Little Boy (he loves baseball because "the same thing happens over and over" [266])—serve to remind us of the novel's pervasive imagery of replication and circularity, imagery upon which the novel's most fundamental vision rests.

"To Replicate Itself Endlessly"

What, then, beyond the vibrant if critically ironic fictionalization of past American life, does this complex narrative voice articulate? Any number of critics have seen in the novel a critical vision that they admire or condemn, while a significant minority have seen no vision at all. "In a novel in which surface counts for so much," Leonard Kriegel mused upon reading *Ragtime,* "the reader suspects that there is something vital underneath. But perhaps there isn't."[34] Indeed, we have earlier seen Greil Marcus argue that the book lacks thematic motive, and agreeing with him, Richard Todd, another hostile critic, argues that "the essential lesson of *Ragtime*'s animated, jagged, syncopated prose is that nothing connects. The book revels in nonsequentiality. It mocks the idea that a human life can become a coherent narrative."[35] Despite considerable praise for its political and social vision, the novel has also been attacked for being sentimental and for being what has been called derisively a "left-wing pastoral."[36] How do we reconcile these widely differing responses?

In the first place, it is perfectly clear that Doctorow has no simply "objective," neutral interest in "our history"; the characters he creates, the historical figures he recreates, and the actual situations he exploits all strongly suggest, as we have pointed out, a satire based on a deeply critical view of the modern development of the United States. The inhuman technology dramatized by Ford, for example, "established the final proposition of the theory of industrial manufacture—not only that the parts of the finished product be interchangeable, but that the men who build the products be themselves interchangeable parts" (155), a proposition dramatized in *Loon Lake*. The capitalism of Morgan, with its emphasis on eccentricity, economic imperialism, and political power, the exploitation of Evelyn Nesbit's sexual appeal, the racism of New Rochelle, the tendency in American culture to place property above human life (producing ambivalence when Walker's car is vandalized), all testify to Doctorow's commitment to alternative social values. However dazzling his portrayal of the ragtime era, then, however aloof the narrator, the novelist is in no sense detached from its significance; he clearly identifies with those writers who accept a collective—as opposed to an individualistic—approach to the writer's responsibility.

But the qualities that cause negative critical reactions like those of Marcus and Todd remain to be accounted for, because the sense in the novel that "nothing connects" is powerful. But the problem here may result from confusing the evocation of a world that lacks sequential and progressive meaning with a work suffering from the same flaw; though the world does not connect, the artist does. Despite, or in contradiction to, the book's political perspective, the novel's deeper, more radical vision is of a world seemingly devoid of meaningful connection, though constantly connected, a world of unending change and simultaneously of continual repetition.

In *Welcome to Hard Times*, Blue, attempting to create and record an ordered world, arrives at the terrifying conclusion and "sudden breathless vision" of his "unending futility" (*Welcome*, 171). Trying to explain the persistence of destructive forces, he concludes that "nothing is ever buried, the earth rolls in its tracks, it never goes anywhere, it never changes, only the hope changes like morning and night, only the expectations rise and set" (*Welcome*, 214). In many ways this is the conclusion that Daniel either arrives at or is in danger of arriving at; however much he studies the past he cannot get beyond the conviction that "everything is elusive" (*Daniel,* 54). In *Ragtime* the recognition of "the violence underlying all principle" (216) produces a novel that at its fundamental level is more descriptive than genuinely diagnostic, hence its basic theme suggests that Doctorow's conflict is more nearly with the nature of things than with American values, however critical he might be of the latter.

In *Ragtime* there is no easily identifiable Blue or Daniel to narrate the story and articulate the negative myth of hopeless repetition; it may be that Doctorow's commitment to social satire demands the inscrutable, impersonal detached voice, the almost mythic artist. But the cyclical images in the novel are everywhere and far too numerous and insistent to be fully detailed here. Freud finds that America is "a gigantic mistake" because it repeats "the chaos of an entropic European civilization" (44). J. P. Morgan is obsessed with endless reincarnation, ironically seen as "universal patterns of order and repetition that give meaning to the activities of this planet" (169). Henry Ford's genius is to create "a machine to replicate itself endlessly" (155). The very plot of the Coalhouse Walker story—roughly a third of the novel—is an uncanny recapitulation of Heinrich von Kleist's 1808 novella *Michael Kohlhaas;* it translates the story of social injustice from sixteenth-century Germany to twentieth-century America, replicating detail after detail.[37] Tateh, having become a rich filmmaker, produces a number of children's movies that look exactly like Hal Roach's famous "Our Gang" series, and Doctorow describes the racially and ethnically mixed cast as "a society of ragmuffins, like all of us, a gang, getting into trouble and getting out again" (369). And Father, killed when a German submarine sinks the *Lusitania,* is seen by the narrator in that sudden shift into first person in terms similar to Daniel's view of "the final existential condition of citizenship" (*Daniel,* 85): "Poor Father, I see his final exploration. He arrives at the new place, his hair risen in astonishment, his mouth and eyes dumb. His toe scuffs a soft storm of sand, he kneels and his arms spread in pantomimic celebration, the immigrant, as in every moment of his life, arriving eternally on the shore of his Self" (368).

The final sentence of the novel shows us the wealthy murderer Harry K. Thaw released from the insane asylum where he had been placed following his trial for killing his wife's lover, marching—ironically—in the first annual Armistice Day parade; like the Bad Man from Bodie in *Hard Times* he has returned, a permanent presence in life. Thus, seemingly in every way, the world composes and recomposes itself.

But perhaps ragtime music itself provides the ultimate metaphor: "the syncopated melodies in the right hand are set over a regular repeating bass in the left."[38] Thus, while the pianist's right hand seemingly ranges in constant improvisation, his left hand produces the constant repetition that must inevitably subdue the illusory freedom of the right hand. Hence, "as the left hand provides a bass line of historical events and narrative movement," Bernard F. Rodgers points out, in *Ragtime* "the right hand furnishes the repetitions."[39] The rich variety of Doctorow's fourth novel is thus played out against a reiterated sameness that is the antithesis of progressive change.

The illusionist—Houdini-Doctorow—can finally discover no meaningful pattern in this endless repetition, and the novel's deepest implications thus challenge the implied social analysis of the novel's surface. Constructive social criticism assumes the possibility of understanding history and of changing behavior and institutions to achieve some better realization of human potential and social justice. But at the heart of *Ragtime,* the fable enacted is, like that of *Hard Times,* one of the repeated undoing of hope. Doctorow's objective may have been what Joseph Moses finds in the work, an intention "to impose a phrasing on history, to syncopate its rhythm—to rag time."[40] But Blue's sad realization in *Hard Times* that "nothing is ever buried" seems to apply to the fundamental experience of *Ragtime* as well. The artist-as-Little Boy knows "that the world composed and recomposed itself constantly in an endless process of dissatisfaction" (135). But if such is the case, art yet remains, and any human being, even a fairly limited one, may come to realize the value to be found in the "contingency of song." (*Drinks,* vi). Facing the blank chaos of the Arctic winter: "Father kept himself under control by writing in his journal. This was a system too, the system of language and conceptualization. It proposed that human beings, by the act of making witness, warranted times and places for their existence other than the time and place they were living through" (83–84). Blue, Creighton, and Daniel would all agree.

Chapter Five

Loon Lake and the
Vision of Synchronicity:
"Exactly Like You"

Because the critical controversy and commercial success of *Ragtime* catapulted Doctorow into instant celebrity, as well as secured his place as a formidable and respected literary personality, the publication of his next novel was awaited with considerable anticipation and excitement. But its actual reception was, at best, mixed. Finally emerging in 1980, five years after *Ragtime, Loon Lake* was received enthusiastically by some and as a confused and confusing disappointment by others. Like many other early reviewers, Robert Towers, for example, admired the novel's virtuosity ("If *Ragtime* is a work of brilliant surfaces, then *Loon Lake* is a work of brilliant parts"[1]), but he also believed the novel failed to achieve "some graspable, salient sense of the whole."[2] On the other end of the critical spectrum, Pearl K. Bell made a very unflattering comparison of *Loon Lake* to John Dos Passos's *U.S.A.*, condemning Doctorow's technical experiments as conveying "little more than the author's hortatory ineptitude."[3] In any case, the novel did not cause the sensation or wide commentary *Ragtime* stimulated, nor has it since been converted into a film, perhaps because it is perceived as too cerebral, too "literary."[4]

While the novel *is* technically difficult—both structurally and stylistically—it nevertheless represents, among other things, another of Doctorow's meditations on American history and, thus adds to the growing body of work that places him squarely in the American literary tradition. Indeed, we will argue, the negative reactions to *Loon Lake* reflect a misunderstanding of both meaning and method and result primarily from a misapprehension of point of view and the unusual structure that is a consequence of Doctorow's manipulation of point of view.

"A Sort of Depression Bildungsroman"

From at least one perspective, however, *Loon Lake* retells a story both Doctorow and a multitude of other American novelists have told before:

"You remember the G.A.P. [the Great American Plot]. An innocent, lonely, ambitious (or proud) hero (or heroine) is corrupted by a callous, hypocritical society. He (she) would have to be nuts to have known better. Expiation is possible, though usually unpleasant. These three sentences may be as easily applied to Hester Prynne, Isabel Archer, Huck Finn, Jay Gatsby, Jake Barnes and Quentin Compson as to the narrator of *Loon Lake*."[5] Like these memorable and by now archetypal figures—his predecessors in the American literary tradition—the protagonist of *Loon Lake*, a boy at first not named, then called simply Joe (or Joe of Paterson) seeks escape from a limited and limiting childhood and goes on a journey—both literal and spiritual—that reveals the best and worst of American life in the Great Depression year of 1936. In the process of pursuing simultaneously several classic American dreams (a golden woman, money, power, and his ultimate desire, fame), the boy is exposed to the full spectrum of American experience according to Doctorow: numbing poverty, gross human exploitation, obscene luxury, callous sexuality, nature unnaturally owned, and a plethora of examples of capitalistic acquisition and consumption. Along the way he also experiences affection, generosity, poetry, and the opportunity to find or create a self. Living by his not inconsiderable wits, he manages, despite the often painful isolation characteristic of the American hero, to forge an identity and, this time in the Horatio Alger and Jay Gatsby tradition, to grasp—by the conclusion of the novel's present—remarkable material success, extraordinary power, and, we infer, the acclaim he tells us early in the narrative is his single-minded goal: "I only wanted to be famous!" (2). In this, its simplest sense, the plot of *Loon Lake* can be described as the classic American version of the bildungsroman.[6]

It would be hard to exaggerate how accurately, and at the same time, how inaccurately, this synopsis both represents and misrepresents Doctorow's fifth novel. For although he very consciously seems to evoke this traditional "Great American Plot," Doctorow does so the same way Joyce evokes the Odysseus myth in *Ulysses* or the way Faulkner uses the biblical story of Benjamin in *The Sound and the Fury*; as a kind of objective correlative, or store-window mannequin on which he will hang the most strikingly original literary costume. Even the plot itself—the naked mannequin—will be twisted and postured in remarkably novel ways. Rarely unfolded in recognizably chronological order, presented in unpredictable arrangements of prose, prose-poetry, "semilyric computerese,"[7] and in short, resumé-like biographical sketches, the story of the central character is nevertheless classically simply.

Beginning with an unequivocal and cold rejection of his working-class par-

ents and their drab lives barely eked out in the gray urban environment of
Paterson, New Jersey, Joe embarks on a life of personal aggrandizement and
adventure. At first conning his way into a series of jobs in New York City, he
uses his wits and considerable ability to play a variety of roles to assure himself of employment, sexual gratification, and money: "I was interested in the
way I instantly knew who the situation called for and became him" (7). In
New York, restlessly absorbing the innumerable tales of the pitiful, but often
eloquent, legions of the unemployed, he hears about the alleged opulence of
a place where "you could eat oranges off the trees" (9) and determinedly
makes California his goal, attempting to get there with the thousands of
other hobos hopping trains and hitchhiking west. Soon after he sets out on
that journey, however, he is temporarily distracted by the fascinating world of
a traveling carnival and its freaks and becomes a roustabout, observing "how
money was made from the poor" (15) and developing grudging respect for
the taciturn carnival owner, Sim Hearn.

Just as he has us hooked into this relatively straightforward, picaresque
narrative, however, Doctorow interrupts the story of Joe to introduce the second major character of the novel, would-be poet Warren Penfield, a man
born—we will discover only at the very end of the novel—on the same day as
Joe, but nineteen years earlier, in 1899. While we learn a good deal about the
facts of Warren's life from a brief vitae inserted into the narrative here, we are
also dramatically introduced to his early life in a coal mining community in
Colorado (about the time of the Ludlow mine disaster of 1910), where the
harsh, deadly existence of immigrant miners parallels the urban impoverishment Joe experienced in Paterson. Unlike Joe, who finds little beauty in his
childhood environment, Warren's romantic and poetic sensibility is immediately apparent in his translation of experience from the brutal to the sensual
and in his obsession with a little girl (the first of three such children-women)
who becomes the embodiment of some personally mythic brand of woman-
hood, "the fruition of a small fertile universe" (12). We learn quickly that
Warren will reject his father's desire that he become a miner and vindicate his
parents' lives by being "an organizer a great union orator a radical a leader of
men out of their living graves of coal" (39); but the clear parallels with Joe's
experience are only hinted at here and will be more fully developed in the
elaborate structural interweaving of the two stories as the novel progresses.

Joe and Warren's lives become directly linked in the next sections of novel
as they meet in the early autumn of 1936 at the isolated mountain estate of F.
W. Bennett, industrialist, financier, owner and sole proprietor of Loon Lake,
of fifty thousand acres[8] of Adirondack woodlands, and of a rustic but luxuri-
ous mountain retreat. Having fled Sim Hearn's carnival after he witnesses a

gross act of gang rape committed against the gentle and retarded Fat Lady, Fanny (an act orchestrated and sold by Hearn to the "rubes" of upstate New York, "something special at end of summer" [148]), Joe travels deep into the forest where he has what is for him an almost mystical experience. Suddenly confronted by an elegantly appointed private train traveling through the woods, he sees a naked, beautiful blond woman "holding up for her examination a white dress on a hanger" and is compelled to follow this "vision of incandescent splendor" (31) wherever it leads. It leads, of course, to Bennett's property where a pack of starving, wild dogs attack Joe and Bennett's staff nurses him through a slow recovery. Warren Penfield, having come to this spot seven years earlier to kill Bennett for his alleged outrages against coalminers and other exploited workers, is now the failed killer and "resident poet" of Loon Lake who befriends Joe and shares the scars he too received from an earlier generation of wild dog: "You're not the only one, I want you to know. They treed me seven years ago when I came here one night—just like you" (79).

Although Warren and Joe appear to have little else in common—the former a man of words, the latter, a man of action—they develop and share an unusually close bond based initially on Warren's willingness to treat Joe as a person, as a recognizable individual with whom he deals in a caring way. Warren's attentions legitimize Joe, perhaps for the first time in his young life: "He has made me his friend, this poet, and I have a presence in the world" (108). They soon come to share something else in the person of Clara Lukacs, the eighteen year old blond beauty on the train whom Warren beds and envisions as one of the three manifestations of his early obsession. Joe learns Clara is a visitor to Loon Lake, originally brought there by Tommy Crapo, gangster and hired "industrial relations" tough, but has left with the unstated understanding that she will serve F. W. Bennett's pleasure for as long as he finds her amusing. While Warren is unaware that Joe's accident was the result of his following his vision of Clara to Loon Lake, he nevertheless introduces the two and makes the assumption that the three of them can form a quasi-platonic ménage à trois. Discovering Clara's desire to escape the boring confines of Loon Lake, and finding it impossible to take any direct action to free her, Warren helps Joe and Clara arrange an escape by persuading Lucinda Bennett, F. W.'s independent wife and famous aviatrix, to "loan" "the two young ones" (130) a rarely driven Mercedes, to which Warren adds a small wad of cash. Taking the private phone number Mr. Bennett has given him in case of future trouble and also taking his good luck largely for granted—"I didn't once reflect on the lately peculiar conforming of life to my desires. I didn't think of Lucinda Bennett's generosity or despair, or Mr. Penfield's, nor even reach the most obvious conclusion: that I was leaving Loon Lake in somewhat better condition than I had come" (135)—Joe spirits Clara away in the night, heading once more for the fantasy paradise of California.

The Picaresque

Although Doctorow does not either indicate chapter numbers or divide the novel into discrete parts or major sections, Joe and Clara's "escape" from Loon Lake forms an implicit conclusion to the first movement of the narrative. Beginning with the next chapter (we note as chapter 21 [139]), the novel alternates between chapters that recapture Warren Penfield's peripatetic past and those that, with one exception (the withheld completion of Joe's traumatic experience in Hearn's carnival), dramatize Joe's peripatetic—and for a time, domestic—"present" in the winter of 1936 and the early spring of 1937. In addition to the chapters that develop the two men's histories, two other chapters serve as critical commentaries on the entire narrative: one analyzes the character of F. W. Bennett in light of prevailing theories about capitalism (chapter 27); the other presents a seven-line letter from Warren in which the poet bequeaths all his papers to Joe who is "what I would want my son to be" (chapter 31, [205]).

The fourteen chapters devoted to Joe and Clara's truncated journey (actually ending in Jacksontown, Indiana), provide the bulk of this section of *Loon Lake* and are a deftly rendered series of vignettes of the sterile and hard life of automobile trim workers in America's heartland. Having sold the Mercedes to avoid pursuit by the law (but nevertheless quickly running out of money), Joe consciously seeks a position with the BENNETT AUTOBODY NUMBER SIX plant in Jacksontown. Temporarily dreaming the dream of domestic bliss where he and his unlikely housewife, Clara, can settle ("And this was where we truly belonged, not on the road but stationary, in one place, working it all out in the hard life" [181]), Joe takes on the mechanistic tasks of the assembly line, working as a "headlight man" and discovers the numbing life of endless repetition implicit in Doctorow's version of industrialized America. Attempting to enrich Clara's analogously routine and drab life, he encourages her to befriend an innocent country wife and next-door neighbor, Sandy James, whose crude braggadocio of a husband, Lyle ("Red"), coaxes Joe into clandestine union meetings where secret strikes—rebellions against F. W. Bennett and his company—are being planned.

This brief respite of domesticity is quickly shattered, however, as Red is revealed to be a Crapo Industrial Services spy, betrayer of the union, and is summarily murdered, while Joe, his ostensible supporter, is badly beaten.

Faced with a grieving widow and her baby, police and gangster interrogations as to his own role in the James affair, and an increasingly sarcastic and dissatisfied Clara, Joe once more plots escape, again to the "great honeypot of lower California" (267). After a series of cryptic encounters with alleged company men and union sympathizers, however, Joe also comes to recognize that the "company," in its Crapo Industrial Services manifestation, is actually responsible for the murder of Red, their own operative, and that he is in potential danger. In a risky act of bravado similar to many others in his life—created on the spur of the moment to protect himself, Sandy James, and Clara (who, in the meantime has driven away in a cream-colored LaSalle with her former lover, Tommy Crapo)—Joe bluffs the company-controlled police into believing that his real role in Jacksontown was to spy on Red James for the company and that he did so at the behest of his "father," F. W. Bennett.

Assuming that the authorities have checked on this incredible deception and that Bennett has somehow, at least implicitly, permitted or encouraged the ruse, Joe sets out for California with Sandy, her baby, a truck full of James's furniture, money from Red's life insurance and company "death benefit" and once more dreams the fragile dream of creating domestic bliss with another partner, this time in "a bungalow under palm trees" (276).

But as they trade in their truck for the more decorous ride on the train to Los Angeles, Joe reads of Lucinda Bennett's plane having been lost in the Pacific. A photograph of the plane clearly shows that Warren Penfield was also a passenger. Leaving the money with the sleeping Sandy and baby, Joe jumps the train to return to Loon Lake where now only he, the prodigal and self-created "son," is left to comfort the despairing and isolated F. W. Bennett.

Interspersed with these fourteen chapters that dramatize Joe's flight west (and his predictable return) are four chapters devoted to the earlier adventures of Warren Penfield, three of which detail his sadly comic exploits in Japan, while the other depicts an episode in Oregon during the "General Strike of Seattle February 6, 1919, the first of its kind in the whole history of the United States of America" (255). The Oregon chapter, coming very late in the novel, simultaneously establishes parallels with Joe's brief union experience in Jacksontown and provides the rationale for Warren's flight to Japan, from which he is ultimately deported as an "undesirable alien" in 1927.

These chapters that dramatize Warren's life prior to his journey to Loon Lake in 1929 are presented as part of an imagined dialogue with Lucinda Bennett on their fatal flight in 1937—a flight that mysteriously ends just in time to call Joe of Paterson back to what will be his patrimony.

The Transformation

The forty-second and last chapter of *Loon Lake* is remarkable in several ways. First, it is the longest chapter in the novel and serves as both climax and coda. It also links and loops together all the major characters, the past and the novel's "present," and infers or summarizes relevant bits of data and events that occur between 1937 and the narrator's—and reader's—present time. Lastly, and most dramatically, it reveals, on the last page, critical information about Joe of Paterson that has been carefully withheld until this point.

Having returned to Loon Lake under the illusion that F. W. Bennett had cooperated in his claim of kinship, Joe assumes he will be quickly accepted as "son," particularly now that Lucinda and Warren are presumed dead. What Joe initially learns, however, is that Bennett never received a confirming call from the Jacksontown authorities and, therefore, shares none of Joe's expectations for a joint future. But Joe is now firmly entrenched in his desire to establish himself as Bennett's "son," and by defending his plan as a charitable act, he will rationalize the deceit—the seduction—he is about to perpetrate: "I will testify to God that he is a human being, that is how, I will save him from wasting away. . . . I will give him hope" (293). And he does, by casting an unforgettable image of himself on Loon Lake: F. W. Bennett falls in love with the artifice of Joe of Paterson, a.k.a. Joseph Korzeniowski, who, in 1941, upon his graduation from college, will become Joseph Paterson Bennett, heir to the entire dynasty, later to be distinguished fighter pilot, Central Intelligence Agency official, diplomat, Master of Loon Lake, and narrator of his own story.

"The Hero of His Own Narration"

Reviewers and critics who are most vocal about the lack of coherence or overarching vision in *Loon Lake* invariably share the perception that there is no singular or unifying view or voice that binds the novel's seemingly disjunct parts, temporal shifts, and narrative styles together. For what begins in the first chapter as an easily accessible "I" narrative is inexplicably interrupted by stilted, alliterative verse of an almost nonsensical kind. These short swatches of mock poetry are then transformed in chapter 2 to computer talk: biographical data is introduced that apparently has nothing to do with the "I" narrator of chapter 1, and images of another character, Warren Penfield, viewing what is for him a highly charged symbolic event, are introduced. Dislocating our sense of time and narrative perspective even further, chapter 3 begins in the third person and quickly shifts—again without apparent purpose—back to the comfortable "I" narrative with which the novel begins, only to repeatedly disappear or be diffused in subsequent chapters, unpredictably reemerging throughout the novel without visible design or plan.

These techniques have led some critics to rail against what is for them a preciousness, a self-conscious literariness, that ultimately has neither artistic nor thematic function or merit. Dean Flower, for example, dismisses the novel succinctly: "Doctorow ought to be arrested for displaying so much technique to no purpose."[9] A bit more charitable in his response, Ronald Curran nevertheless finds problems of integration directly attributable to "confusion about point of view and intention."[10] Moreover, there are all sorts of contradictory descriptions of point of view in the novel, although most critics seem to accept as fact something similar to Alan Brownjohn's claim that "The narrative of *Loon Lake* is divided between Joe and Penfield."[11] In addition to identifying two distinct narrators, several commentators also attribute some of the historical data to "ruminations in the author's own voice" and the computer entries to "various authorial intrusions."[12] Given this fragmented sense of the novel, it is little wonder many critics echo Curran's conclusion that *Loon Lake* "remains an interesting and ambitious fiction that doesn't put its themes and characters very smoothly together."[13]

What becomes increasingly clear from a close, and probably second or third reading of the novel, is that Joe Paterson Bennett is in fact the single narrator and controlling consciousness of *Loon Lake*. Although we cannot know this at the beginning of the narrative—and only fully apprehend both this fact and its significance at the very end of the novel—we begin to see that only Joe has literal or imaginative access to all the players and to the many tangible materials that will inform the entire narrative. Like the narrator of *Ragtime*, Joe is a collector of sources of information: he listens to and absorbs Warren's poetry (in both oral and written form) and inherits all "papers, copies of chapbooks, letters, *pensées*, journals, night thoughts—all that is left of me" (205) from him. Joe thereby comes to "possess" the raw materials necessary to dramatize Warren Penfield very directly. He is able to assume Warren's "voice" and does so in the chapters devoted to him: "I augment my memory with the lines actually printed in a private edition" (96). Even when we are presented with what is ostensibly Warren's unedited *vers libre*, we are reading an "annotated text" (57), a text that Joe has in his possession and that is now subject to his control and shaping. Joe is annotator.

As the story progresses, Joe the narrator begins to reveal himself and describe his methods. Glimpsing Clara for the first time, for example, Joe has a curious reaction that signals his heightened sensitivity to words, to language: "Into my vacated mind flowed all the English I never knew I'd learned at

Paterson Latin High School. Grammar slammed into my brain" (31). Recreating the episode where he is attacked by wild dogs, he divulges his capacity not only for language, but for invention: "Now I'll tell what I don't remember" (46). Creating a scene in what we think is Clara's consciousness, Joe tells us: "But it was all in my mind, it was the furthest thing from everyone's mind except mine" (282). Even when he is focusing on another character altogether he gives us a clue to what has gradually become his purpose: "I thought this was about Clara it is not it is about my life" (250).

But Doctorow purposely delays our discovery that Joe is solely responsible for the narration; he creates a form of "mystery" with a progressively unfolding solution: "In 'Loon Lake' the narrator throws his voice, and the reader has to figure out who and what he is."[14] That there is a single narrator is therefore revealed only as Joe acquires the essential materials, sensibility, and self-consciousness to become what he knows he has learned to become from Warren: "the hero of his own narration" (260). And the transformation from crass urban picaro to complex human being and artist is not complete when he becomes F. W. Bennett's "son" in the spring of 1937, but rather continues for the next forty years. For the man who creates this narrative has developed parallel lives somewhat akin to Wallace Stevens's public life as an insurance executive and his private life as a remarkably sensuous poet. Here, Joseph Bennett has assumed the dualistic persona of his two spiritual fathers: his public and professional life replicates and extends F. W. Bennett's; his personal, very private life, manifests the artistic legacy of Warren Penfield. But even as artist he incorporates the tools of his public life and trade: he uses the computer to embody the mechanistic values of modern capitalistic society, producing parodies of poetry—another kind of "industrial manufacture of [his] own" (263)—and he reproduces biographical files, perhaps representative of those accessible only to the highly placed CIA official we learn he has been. Gathered all together—the remnants of memory, the poems and papers of Penfield, the possessions and "freedom" of Bennett, the files and knowledge of an intelligence expert, the versatile computer—all these bits and pieces available exclusively to Joseph Paterson Bennett form the grist of art that he will organize as best he can "for rendering nonlinear thinking in linear language, the apperceptions of oneness in dualistic terminology" (158). In other words, the radical nature of the narrative Joe assembles is his attempt to replicate nonsequentially experienced, felt life—a sophisticated form of the imitative fallacy, for which he says ironically, "your register apologizes" (158).

Again using the metaphor of the ventriloquist, Doctorow describes his own method in *Loon Lake*: "It is more like *Daniel* in being a discontinuous narrative with deferred resolutions, and in the throwing of multiple voices that turn out to be the work of one narrator."[15] What this ventriloquist—this master of disguises and false identities—will learn and reveal in the course of telling his tale forms the existential experience that is at the center of *Loon Lake*.

American Dreams, American Romance

More than almost any other recent American novel, *Loon Lake* is invariably and insistently compared to other American literary classics. Although *U.S.A.* and *The Great Gatsby* are most often mentioned, the list of works to which Doctorow's strikingly (and ironically, in this context) original novel is compared—sometimes favorably and sometimes condescendingly—is impressive indeed; a casual review of the allusions reveals the following: *An American Tragedy, An American Dream, Goodbye, Columbus, Moby Dick, The Grapes of Wrath, Paterson, Walden, All the King's Men, Pale Fire,* "Diamond as Big as the Ritz," Whitman's poetry, and the Horatio Alger stories. What seems to motivate these comparisons is the sense of classic American terrain and themes revisited and, in this regard, Doctorow should no doubt be flattered by the company he is presumed to keep.

As anyone at all familiar with the man and his work is well aware, Doctorow is deeply conscious of both his debt to the great American masters and his fascination with history, particularly American history. And he recognizes in the very brevity and tentativeness of our history a unique opportunity to be creative in its interpretation, reinterpretation, even its "invention": "We don't have much of a history—that's the simple, statistical fact of it" (*EC*, 58). He also sees the American past as full of possibility for the fabulator, for it offers creative options not easily available in other cultures: "Not having fixed, narrowed or focused into a real, true national identity, we can have the illusion about ourselves that we are still in the process of becoming. It's a kind of fascinating suspense" (*EC*, 58). This sense of existing in "the process of becoming" informs the original ways Doctorow approaches all American history in his novels, but is particularly apropos to *Loon Lake*, where Joe's (and, to a lesser extent, each of the other character's) quest, both literally and figuratively, is to become someone—someone very specifically American. Thus, at the first level of simple American Dream myths, Joe's life represents—and the novel's structure reinforces—the formula that Saltzman reminds us is: "the 'get-rich-quick' optimism of Horatio Alger, whose tales of virtuous innocents receiving astounding rewards imagine an America of infinite promise and generosity" (*EC*, 100).

But what makes Joe's journey so profoundly different from Horatio Alger characters—or others (like Jay Gatsby or J. P. Morgan in *The Great Gatsby* and *Ragtime*) who partake in the materialistic and power-oriented aspects of the American Dream—is not only the process he goes through to arrive there, but the self-consciousness with which he is able to choose—actually to will into being—that end. For Joe is offered several options along the way, options that themselves represent alternative American Dreams. He can get to California and have the middle-class dream of "a bungalow under palm trees, something made of stucco with a red tile roof. I thought of the warm sun. I imagined myself driving up to my bungalow in the palm trees, driving up in an open roadster and tooting the horn as I pulled up to the curb" (276); he can live on the fringes of society as a roustabout, a hobo, a union organizer, a poet-in-residence. But these American Dreams do not place one in history it-self, do not permit one to sign the Loon Lake guest book wherein a kind of crude immortality is realized. As Joe contemplates that guest book at a time when he knows little of himself (except that he wanted "to be famous"), he thinks: "I felt I could learn something, that there was something here, some powerful knowledge I could use. But it was in code! If only I could under-stand the significance of the notations, I'd have what I needed I'd know what I'd always dreamed of knowing—although I couldn't have said what it was. I touched the signatures. . . . It was some mysterious system of legalities and caste and extended brilliant endeavor" (75). That he seeks a self that will place him in *history* is not yet at all obvious; this will become increasingly ap-parent as he tries on and discards other American identities.

Finally rejecting the option of remaining on the assembly line in Jacksontown, for example, Joe begins, perhaps for the first time, to de-velop some conscious recognition of choice and goals: "I wanted to shake this cement cast from my bones as I wanted to shake free of this weight of local life and disaster. None of it was mine, I thought, none of it was justly mine. . . . I wanted to be back at my best, out of everyone's reach, in flight. But I had all this weight and I felt . . . there was hardly time for what I had to do in order to lift it from me so that we could get free" (232). Freedom, flight, the weight of the cast (caste) lifted and fame; these are the qualities of being Joe will pursue.

In this sense, then, Joe is a romantic and his dream, paralleled by Warren Penfield's, is to transcend the bounds of success in either traditional, or even more radical, American terms. While this wish for flight and transcendence is embodied in many ways in the novel—particularly in the analogous meta-phors of the loon and of Lucinda's plane (where Warren fittingly dies in his final flight)—it also incorporates the quest for the idealized woman, which

Joe and Warren share to a remarkable degree, as the repeated vision of a beautiful baby girl urinating attests. That this image reappears in both Warren's and Joe's memories may be a product of Joe the narrator's conflation of their seemingly synchronous experiences; in any case, it comes to represent their parallel obsessions—Warren's with the three children-women he will love (the girl in Ludlow, Clara, and the Japanese "child bride in the Zen garden") and Joe's with Clara (a lower-class version of Gatsby's Daisy). That the images both men evoke are virtually identical in their apparent fertility (urine transforming Warren's rural dust into "instantly formed minuscule tulips" [12] on the one hand, and Joe's urban tar into a substance that "shone clearer than a night sky" [131] on the other), suggests the romantic origins of their mutual fantasy. That neither of them will more than temporarily possess such a woman—or father children when they do (a fact that will be coldly registered by the CIA-like notation, "no issue")—suggests another way in which the romantic quest is ironically treated by Doctorow. Having betrayed or been betrayed by all the mother figures in his life (his biological mother, the Scandinavian maid, Magda Hearn, Sandy James, Fanny), Joe will relinquish his desire to find an idealized love and accept the Bennett legacy of nonfruitful marriages to society women where love "wasn't a feeling at all but a simple characterless state of shared isolation" (272).

Likewise, the American Dream of money plays a particularly ambiguous role in *Loon Lake*. For as it does in much of Doctorow's earlier work, money—and its megasource, capitalism—is clearly a corrupting force. Bennett's company pays "settlement" dollars to miners' widows, Joe's biological parents, and to Sandy James when Red is murdered. In each case Bennett is exchanging blood money for lives he has ended or could be accused of having ended. Moreover, "all the sexual relationships involve money," as Diane Johnson notes in a brilliant essay, and "are developed in sadistic and economic terms."[16] Joe initially has no compunction about stealing silver from the house in which a grateful maid has eagerly accepted his sexual favors. Clara is repeatedly "bought" in one way or another, by Tommy Crapo, by Bennett, and even by Joe, who provides her shelter, protection, and movie magazines in exchange for her affections.

But while Joe at first seems to be comfortable in this mode of economic exchange, he is also capable of forcefully rejecting it. Leaving Sandy James to the middle-class dream, he also tucks "the fat wallet with her death benefits under her chin" (292), taking only a few dollars on which to survive. Earlier, when a priest apprehends him for robbing a poor box, Joe screams: "take your fucking money and rearing back throw it to heaven run under it as it rains down pennies from heaven on the stone floor ringing like chaos loosed on the good stern Father" (4). Here, rejection of money symbolizes Joe's repudiation of religion and of one of the several false "fathers" he will disavow in his search for paternity. In an even more critical scene—repeated almost verbatim in two sections of the novel (27 and 151)—Joe casts the ill-gotten gains of Fanny's death-rape into the winds after he has sexually abused Magda Hearn ("the coins sticking to the wet ass, the wet belly" [151]) for her crass acceptance of Fanny's exploitation: "With all my might I reared back and threw the bills into the wind. I thought of them as the Fat Lady's ashes" (151).

The simple possession of money, then, is never Joe's goal because he unconsciously recognizes that it often represents either betrayal or death, or both. That he later desires and accepts wealth is related not to greed or to the acquisition of possessions qua possessions, but to the recognition that wealth simultaneously creates freedom and isolation, the two conditions that most represent his existential (and ultimately, artistic) sense of self: "there was some faculty of being alone I was born with . . . my brain was alone in the silence of observation and perception and understanding" (3). Immediately cognizant of similar qualities in Bennett, Joe sees the ambiguity of "the frightening freedom of him" (121); he also projects his awareness of the value of wealth in the sequence he invents for Clara: "So at last she understands what wealth is, the desire for isolation, its greatest achievement is isolation, its godliness is in its isolation" (281). That he will so unequivocally reject his working-class background and will choose this isolation—and in so doing firmly reject the American Dream of the left, the Dream of solidarity and community—leads many commentators to the conclusion that "Joe's rise in the world is Joe's capitulation to the world."[17] Or, extending the Oedipal metaphor, George Stade argues, "In *Loon Lake*, Joe of Paterson (or Father-Son) triumphs over his adoptive father by becoming him, only worse. . . . In America . . . the sons win; they destroy the past only to preserve the worst of it in themselves, and thereby destroy the future. Such is Doctorow's variation on the conventional American success story."[18] These socially acceptable interpretations—implicitly acknowledging Doctorow's rarely disguised personal politics—do not, however, accurately represent the novel's multiple ambiguities or its paradoxical conclusion, just as similar statements do not acknowledge the dualism found in *Daniel*.

"Joseph Korzeniowski"

Although a multitude of American dreams and myths are evoked by Doctorow in *Loon Lake*, and although the experimental techniques used in the novel often, and no doubt intentionally, recall those employed by Dos Passos in *U.S.A.*, the most startling literary allusion occurs on the last page of the novel, when, for the first time, Joe reveals what he has referred to before as his "unpronounceable" given name: "Herewith bio Joseph Korzeniowski" (294). Whereas several critics recognize the unmistakable reference to Joseph Conrad's Polish surname, few believe its inclusion in *Loon Lake* is anything but gratuitous. Again displaying her impatience with what she believes are Doctorow's literary pretensions, Pearl Bell calls the use of Conrad's name "a whimsical in-joke signifying nothing,"[19] while Geoffrey Harpham merely footnotes the allusion, calling it "the most intriguing literary reference in the text,"[20] but not developing that notion except to mention a few of Conrad's suggestive titles such as "The Secret Sharer," *The Secret Agent*, and *The Mirror of the Sea*. Doctorow, when asked why he had used the name, said teasingly, "perhaps to confound the Ph.D.s" (*DOP*, 195).

Careful craftsman that he is, however, one cannot dismiss Doctorow's use—and purposeful withholding—of the name as insignificant or gratuitous, for he has spent a goodly portion of the novel exploring the myths and realities of paternity, of identity, and of the creating, the naming, and renaming of self in the embodiment of Joe of Paterson. He has also developed in the unfolding narrative a mystery of identity whose final resolution is only possible when all the pieces of the puzzle are put into place by the self-reflexive, self-conscious narrator. In this light, therefore, Doctorow's evocation of Conrad's real name, whatever his intention, reinforces, completes, and extends our understanding of both the identity and experience of the narrator. For, like Conrad, Joe of Paterson is a man of many identities: whereas Conrad was a Polish expatriot turned seaman turned English family man and novelist, Joe is a working-class American turned picaro turned the American equivalent of an "aristocrat" turned, finally like Conrad, artist. Whereas Conrad was himself a youthful adventurer smuggling guns to Carlist conspirators in Spain and later writing about international revolutionaries and government spies in *The Secret Agent* and *Under Western Eyes*,[21] Joseph Paterson Bennett will be an army intelligence officer "parachuting into France in black sweater flight jacket trousers black boots false passport black wool cap . . . heart blackened dropping into blackness" (294), then a CIA official, then an ambassador, and finally a writer.

Moreover, the subjects and manipulations of complex narrative structures also suggest parallels between Conrad and Joe Korzeniowski-Doctorow: the frequent obsession with the doppelgänger, most obvious in "The Secret Sharer" but also apparent in much of Conrad's mature work, echoes in the counterpointing experiences of Warren and Joe. But perhaps most important is the role of Conrad's perceptive and inscrutable narrator, Marlow. Just as Warren seeks (although unsuccessfully) peace and enlightenment in Japan through Buddhism, Marlow—in his superior knowledge gained through the observation of life and the telling of tales—seems to have found it: "he . . . sat apart, indistinct and silent, in the pose of a meditating Buddha."[22] It is perhaps Marlow, narrator not only of *Heart of Darkness*, but also of "Youth," *Lord Jim*, and *Chance*, who Doctorow most wants us to envisage when he invokes Conrad. For through the experiences of others, Marlow comes to profound knowledge that he repeatedly communicates through his several narratives: "Droll thing life is—that mysterious arrangement of merciless logic for a futile purpose. The most you can hope from it is some knowledge of yourself—that comes too late—a crop of unextinguishable regrets."[23] Although Joe's choice of the Bennett name and legacy would seem to make him Marlow's opposite number, his convoluted telling of the tale may well represent knowledge gained through a trip into his own heart of darkness. For unlike the Bennett he has chosen to emulate, Joe is retrospectively self-analytical and self-critical. Describing himself in the third person, for instance: "he was not unmindful that his life since leaving Paterson had been a picaresque of other men's money and other men's women" (272). Or musing about his adult values, he is clearly cognizant of the transitory nature of life: "I mourn all change even for the better" (284). The Conrad allusion, therefore, becomes functional and important to a full understanding of the novel when we view it as a clue to Joe as narrator, who is able to distance himself—as Marlow is—from experience in order to make implicit, but self-revealing, judgments about the life he has lived. That Conrad himself was an extraordinarily conservative man and moralist may reflect on Doctorow's own developing human and aesthetic—if not political—values.[24]

"Our Simultaneous but Disynchrous Lives"

In what is perhaps the single most perceptive short study of Doctorow's narrative vision and its manifestations in *The Book of Daniel, Ragtime*, and *Loon Lake*, Geoffrey Galt Harpham makes the following assertion: "In his last three books Doctorow has retold the same story, about a boy who finds himself in an unacceptable narrative determined by the wills of others and who gradually acquires the skills to form his own narrative."[15] As this insightful statement about novels that appear to be totally dissimilar illustrates, Harpham is one of the few students of Doctorow's work who recognizes how much this seemingly "political" writer is also interested in epistemological and aesthetic questions and in the relationship of these questions to each other, to history, to issues of personal identity, and to the struggles of the artist and his artist characters. And while Harpham focuses on the often very technical aspects of his art, he also understands that Doctorow's continual interest in narrative is not solely the abstract or purely metafictional interest of many of his contemporaries but is indeed ultimately a symbol for fundamental humanistic concerns: "Earlier I said that Doctorow's central continuing concern was narrative, but it seems equally just to say that he has always been concerned with the conditions of the self."[26]

We would argue that Doctorow is *primarily* interested in the "conditions of the self" and that the ability to define, objectify, and thereby to understand the "self" and its relation to the world is intimately related to the ability to create narrative. While we have already seen this principle in its most straightforward form in Blue's ledger writing and, in a more complex way, in Daniel's multidimensional experiments with narrative, it approaches its most intricate—and perhaps most profoundly self-conscious—manifestation in *Loon Lake*. For Joe does not simply "acquire the skills to form his own narrative," to create an artifact; Joe *is* an artifact and, by so being, symbolizes the power of art and language to create a transubstantiation of a potential self into a very specific and a very "*privileged* self, the subject of history."[27] At the very moment Joe discovers this power (when he is about to claim publicly that he is Bennett's son), he begins the process of becoming an artist of the self, a process that will last a lifetime: "I had found a voice to give authority to the claim I was making—without knowing what that claim would be, I had found the voice for it, I listened myself to the performance as it went on" (260). Dimly recognizing the ability simultaneously to invent and to stand outside the self (which will later translate into alternating uses of the first and third person when describing himself), Joe also connects the process directly to art: "I had learned the basics from my dead friend Lyle James. But the art of it from Mr. Penfield, yes, the hero of his own narration with life and sun and stars and universe concentrically disposed on the locus of his tongue—pure Penfield" (260). And then, in an almost Joycean epiphany, Joe connects art to existence itself: "I was going to make it! This was survival at its secret source, and no amount of time on the road or sentimental education could have brought me to it if the suicidal boom of my stunned heart didn't threaten my extinction" (264). Here Joe has discovered his ability to create his own genealogy; and, in so doing, he has created a mythic self with a past, here a present, and for the next forty years, a future based entirely on the artifice of self-generated invention.

What Joe will later discern is how helpless he is to extend the uses of art to reproduce the processes and experiences of life. Having created a self so apparently successfully, he creates the narrative we are reading—this text—to capture affective experience, but learns, much as Blue and Daniel did, that the sequential nature of language and even of radically unorthodox narrative arrangements cannot replicate life. Using every "technique" he can muster—particularly the computer that has the revolutionary capacity to transcend sequence through its spatial "memory" (and through the "perfect mobility of its text"[28])—he tries to arrange experiences, images, facts, words, and "data" that reflect life as it is lived and embody the human desire for connectedness and unity, for reciprocal understanding. If human feelings and experiences are inherently similar, shared, and repetitive, meaning is possible and perceptible. That explains why Joe is so quickly attracted to Warren. For Warren is not only the source of artistic possibility for Joe, he is also a believer in synchronicity: "perhaps we all reappear, perhaps all our lives are impositions one on another" (205). Using his art to create that synchronicity—by becoming himself another Bennett, by spatially and poetically merging his and Warren's visions and experiences, and by repeatedly using mechanical images that reinforce the interchangeability of parts—Joe attempts to make Warren's sense of artistic potential immanent. For Warren has earlier told Joe that "I spend my life understanding feelings, yes, my own and others, that's what I do, that's what poets do, that's what they're supposed to do" (77). But what Joe seems to conclude at the very end of his narrative is that Warren was deluded when he assumed that "My pain is your pain. My life is your life" (130). There is no such interconnectedness to life, only to narrative, narrative that cannot replicate experience: "You are thinking it is a dream. It is no dream. It is the account in helpless linear translation of the unending love of our simultaneous but disynchrous lives" (291). The vision of synchroncity is an illusion; we may live our lives simultaneously, in whole or in part, but they remain separate, unattached, unharmonized. We are all isolated. Only in and through art—by definition, an optimistic act—does the often repeated refrain and the sentiment to be "exactly like you" have meaning. Although the result of a far more sophisticated mind and process, Joe's insight echoes Blue's: "I have the cold feeling everything I've written doesn't tell how it was, no matter how careful I've been to get it all down it still escapes me . . . have I showed the sand shifting under our feet, the terrible arrangement of our lives?" (*Hard Times*, 203).

"Urban Romantic"

One of the primary devices Joe-Doctorow uses to create a vision of synchronicity is his arrangement and evocation of images that have or come to have a shared set of associations between and among the major actors in the drama. The loon itself and the quiet isolated lake named after it are, of course, among the central images around which Joe the narrator (at one time strictly an urban dweller) structures his story. That the lake is cold, still, and uninviting is not a function of an insensitive lack of appreciation for the natural world, but rather an expression of Joe's recognition that this is nature wholly owned and controlled by one man, F. W. Bennett: "wilderness as luxury" (49). Because he has never lived in a natural setting before, Joe initially has no experiential knowledge of such a place, nor does he have a preconceived romantic vision of it; indeed, he wanders on to Bennett's property because he is following Clara and the private train—a symbol of urban life and modern technology. That his first experience of Bennett's retreat is to suffer an attack by wild, vicious dogs does nothing to romanticize the setting or its associations.

Warren—likewise attacked by an earlier version of these same dogs—also comes to perceive Loon Lake and its environs as a symbol not of peace or natural goodness, but as an extension of Bennett's oppressive wealth and power. In the poem he allegedly writes and leaves to Joe (we cannot know to what extent the mature Joe has annotated it), titled "Loon Lake," Warren interweaves a vision of primeval times when "Indians of Loon Lake / the Adirondack nations" (58) lived "a clear cold life" with contrasting images of the visit of Tommy Crapo and Clara's gang to Bennett's retreat where, in a "long mahogany Chris-Craft" (61) the group takes a boat ride, desecrating the lake with mechanical speed and unlit cigarettes and "even the land they couldn't see / under the water / was what he owned" (62). In this context, then, nature becomes unnatural. As Diane Johnson observes, "Nature itself is an aspect of social injustice. . . . Nature is ice is capitalism. Loon Lake is 'a cold black lake,' owned, loons preying on fish there, the shores haunted by the ghosts of dying Indians. It is a reflex of capitalist society and a form of selfish luxury. To the urban romantic, like Doctorow, the romantic poet of nature is a poseur."[29]

Embedded in the purposefully paradoxical imagery of nature is the central metaphor of the loon, at first a nameless bird to urban Joe (45), then "a kind of grebe" (51), then a mysterious presence whose behavior is at first inexplicable: "The wind rose in a sudden gust about my ears, and as I looked back to the lake, a loon was coming in like a roller coaster. He hit the water and skidded for thirty yards, sending up a great spray, and when the water settled he was gone. I couldn't see him, I thought the fucker had drowned. But up he popped, shaking and mauling a fat fish. And when the fish was polished off, I heard a weird maniac cry coming off the water, and echoing off the hills" (83). It is only when Warren recites his poem to the young Joe, however, that

Joe begins to imbue the bird with poetic and existential meaning, meaning he recognizes as a function of art, of "the simple giving of words, so moving to this scruffy boy" (96). Later, as narrator, the adult Joe quotes directly from the poem that *he* has printed (and annotated?) in memory of Warren: "Third volume of verse *Loon Lake* unpaged published posthumously by the Grebe Press, Loon Lake NY 1939. No reviews" (22):

> A doomed Indian would hear them at night
>   in their diving
> and hear their cry not as triumph or as rage
> or the insane compatibility with the earth
> attributed to birds of prey
> but in protest against falling
> of having to fall into that black water
> and struggle up from it again and again
> the water kissing and pawing and whispering
> the most horrible promises
> the awful presumptuousness of the water
> squeezing the eyes out of the head
> floating the lungs out on the beak which clamps
>   on them
> like wriggling fish
> extruding all organs and waste matter
> turning the bird inside out
> which the Indian sees is what death is
> the environment exchanging itself for the being.
>   (59)

To the original inhabitants of this unspoiled place, the loon's deathlike dive is symbolic of the natural order of things, the cyclical process whereby death and life are simple exchanges of matter and the loon's cry is in protest to the struggle. What the image comes to mean for Joe, however, is far more complex, for he associates the loon with the struggle for transcendence and rebirth and often ironically attaches that symbolism not only to himself, but to Lucinda Bennett (an almost disembodied figure), to Warren, and even—in his imaginary evocation of her consciousness—to Clara. Immediately after Joe recalls his reading about Lucinda and Warren's disappearance in her plane, *The Loon* (278), he begins the next—and last—chapter of his narrative with: "Images of falling through space through sky through dreams through floor downstairs down well down hole downpour. . . . The cry of loons once heard is not forgotten" (279). Switching to the imagined consciousness of Clara, he creates the link between Lucinda's plane and the loon, the former seeking transcendence only to find death: "she watches . . . two wakes widening behind the pontoons of the airplane finally losing the chase like porpoises turning back underwater as the green-and-white plane exchanges one environment for another and rising slowly turns, twists in the air rising . . . and when she blinks it is gone altogether" (280).

In contrast to Lucinda and Warren who seek transcendence by escaping from life, Joe will attempt forcefully to engage in life just as the loon does when it struggles to return from the black water "up from it again and again" (59). For it is by casting himself in the image of the indomitable loon that Joe seals his and Bennett's bond and forges his identity: "I stand poised on the edge and dive into the water. With powerful strokes learned in the filth of industrial rivers Joe swims a great circle crawl in the sweet clear cold mountain lake. He pulls himself up on the float and stands panting in the sun, his glistening white young body inhaling the light, the sun healing my scars my cracked bones my lacerated soul. . . . Up on the hill Bennett stands on his terrace, a tiny man totally attentive. He has seen the whole thing, as I knew he would. He waves at me. I smile my white teeth. I wave back" (294). Self-consciously moving back and forth between the first and third person, clearly understanding both the deception and triumph of the moment, Joe the narrator has here become the loon in rebirth, the mountain version of the phoenix, the risen Icarus.

That *Loon Lake* embodies a vision of nature corrupted by ownership— "the wilderness as luxury"—cannot be disputed. That Joe's becoming Bennett's heir and ultimately "Master of Loon Lake" signals an unequivocal denunciation of Joe's life—"the ultimate betrayal in terms of the novel's values" as one critic deems it[30]—is far less certain. For Doctorow, Joe may be described more aptly as an ironic counterpart of Thoreau, recognizing that the loon and his Walden Pond offer an isolation and freedom from which the mysteries of existence can be explored through the artistic process and that only "the failure of perception is what did you in" (250).

"Artist as Judge"

Although she finds Doctorow predictable and sometimes tiresome in his social and political themes (and in his "faith in his version of American history"[31]), Diane Johnson nevertheless labels him "one of the bravest and most interesting of modern American novelists, flying in the face of the self-indulgent fashion for confession to write *about* something, reviving the discredited function of artist as judge, and working to find the forms for

judgment."[32] And unlike others who see only the negative consequences of
Joe Korzeniowski's adopting the Bennett persona and legacy, Johnson is cognizant of the ambiguity of that judgment in *Loon Lake*: "even the bad Joe en-
dears himself by his felicitous phrases, by his complexity, and by the splendid
intelligence his author can't help giving him."[33]

In their zeal to embrace him as a "radical Jewish humanist" (*EC*, 109–19)
or as a devotee of Norman O. Brown or Marx (*EC*, 120–49), critics more
often interested in the polemical than in the artistic fail to see how often
Doctorow engages our sympathies with the least proletarian of characters.
On the contrary, the most interesting of Doctorow's complex themes and existential questions are embodied in characters about whom he makes us feel
the most ambivalent—characters who, paradoxically, do *not* represent the
egalitarian values with which Doctorow is usually associated. Blue, for example, is an unregenerate capitalist; Daniel, a sometimes sadistic, and certainly
cruel egoist; and Tateh, is an artist and an immigrant Jew who sells out to the
lures of Hollywood entertainments and materialism. On the surface, Joseph
Paterson Bennett, too, becomes, in many ways, merely a culmination of similarly negative aspects of American culture and life and would seem thereby to
represent the ironically inverted fulfillment of the American Dream.
Doctorow's sense of human complexity is, however, rarely so simple. Recognizing the inherent ironies in these portraits and especially in Joe, Doctorow
nonetheless argues that "Joe writes a lament, basically a song of remorse. The
book is about loss. Novelists are not politicians" (*DOP*, 188).

For example, the odd chapter 27 (183–86) begins with the computerlike
biographical file on F. W. Bennett: "Data comprising life F. W. Bennett un-
dergoing review. Shown in two instances twenty-five years apart" (183).
Often seen as a bitterly ironic "defense" of capitalism and of the excesses to
which Bennett (and presumably Joe in his parallel adulthood) has suc-
cumbed, the chapter's tone and content actually form a more paradoxical
statement. Listing a series of Bennett's most outrageous exploitations, for example, the narrator suggests that we examine "countervailing data re his apparent generosity to worthless poet scrounge and likely drunkard Warren
Penfield. A hint too of his pride in Lucinda Bailey Bennett's aviation achievements. A heart too for spunky derelict kids" (183). Proceeding with an exco-
riating tongue-in-cheek apology for "the class of which Mr. F. W. Bennett is a
member," Joe nevertheless makes several salient points about the relative
"standards of life" and "extraordinary achievement of American civilization"
(185), points that only one totally unfamiliar with Doctorow's recent statements on this subject could find unequivocally ironic. For Doctorow is disil-
lusioned with *all* economic and political systems, as he made perfectly clear in

an interview during the period in which he was writing *Loon Lake*: "But certainly everything else [except anarchism] has been totally discredited: capitalism, communism, socialism. None of it seems to work. No system, whether it's religious or anti-religious or economic or materialistic, seems to be invulnerable to human venery and greed and insanity" (*EC*, 65).

What Doctorow ultimately focuses on in this curious chapter is, once again, Joe's ability to stand outside what he and Bennett represent as members of an economic "class" and to critique the failures of that class and its abuses of power at the same time as he perceives the very particular qualities of the individuals who inhabit that world: "No claim for the perfection of F. W. Bennett, only that like all men he was of his generation and reflected his times in his person. . . . Note is made here too that this man had a boyhood, after all, woke in the astonishment of a bedsheet of sap suffered acne had feelings which frightened him and he tried to suppress was cruelly motivated by unthinking adults perhaps rebuffed or humiliated by a teacher these experiences are not the sole prerogative of the poor poverty is not a moral endowment and a man who has the strength to help himself can help others" (185–86). Personal experience serves to level class and economic distinctions and Joe is ultimately attracted as much to the suffering man F. W. Bennett is as to the abstract power he represents: "I had seen his kingdom and I appreciated him almost more for the distracted humanity he displayed, broken as easily as anyone by simple events. For men all over the country he was, finally, a condition of their life. Yet he wandered about here in his grief, caring for nothing, barely raising his head when the phone rang" (285).

Although at the moment Joe determines he will force Bennett into accepting him as his "son," he rationalizes what he will do as an act of revenge on "this pompous little self-idolator, I'm going to put the fucker where he belongs" (293), he simultaneously acknowledges the renewal of life he will be offering: "I will testify to God that he is a human being. . . . I will save him from wasting away. I will save him from crumbling into a piece of dried shit, into a foul eccentric, you see, I will give him hope, I will extend his reign, I will raise him and do it all so well with such style that he will thank me, thank me for growing in his heart his heart bursting his son" (293).

So while Doctorow does indeed condemn the oppressive uses of capitalistic power in *Loon Lake*, the novel nevertheless transcends political concerns to focus on the affective lives of individuals whose class is finally irrelevant. That Joe acquires economic well-being and power is paradoxical; his choice is potentially corrupting, but it is also liberating, for he acquires the freedom to be continuously self-creating and the isolation to contemplate and write about the ambiguities of self-invention and of "the unending love of our si-

multaneous but disynchrous lives" (291). Doctorow has admitted his own
need for solitude as basic to the artist's role, acknowledging the contradiction
between the need to be politically engaged and the "separation that is required for the writer" (*DOP*, 189).

At the conclusion of his study, Harpham keenly observes; "As Doctorow
becomes more alive to the possibilities for self-invention, he has begun to
conceive of his art in nearly capitalistic terms, confessing his enthusiasm for
'the American entrepreneurial sense of novel writing.'"[34] Perhaps
Doctorow—now a wealthy public figure ("the privileged self, the subject of
history") as a result of the stunning success of *Ragtime*—has discovered quite
personally that "poverty is not a moral endowment" and that however much
he believes the passion of his calling requires a sense of engagement in the
community, the artistic act ultimately transcends the historical and the political. In any case, with *Lives of the Poets* and *World's Fair*, his writing continues
to expand the limits of narrative and to explore the "conditions of self."
Doctorow remains the independent witness.

Chapter Six

"A Mind Looking for Its Own Geography": *Drinks before Dinner, Lives of the Poets,* and *World's Fair*

In many ways, *Loon Lake* pushed out the limits of the "traditional" novel as far as its form would allow and still accommodate Doctorow's literary zeitgeist. Having experimented in that novel with virtually every structural and linguistic device available to him, Doctorow seems to have turned his considerable intellectual and artistic energy to finding not only new voices, but new forms, as his various forays into other creative endeavors—screenwriting, essay writing, collaborative work with a photographer[1]—suggest. It should come as no surprise, then, that, while he was apparently finishing the writing of *Loon Lake* in the late 1970s, he was simultaneously experimenting with new modes of literary expression and, *Drinks before Dinner*, an experimental drama, was the initial result. First produced on 22 November 1978 at the New York Shakespeare Festival, the play was published, with the author's revealing introduction, in 1979.[2]

But the experiment with dramatic form is not the only unusual thing about *Drinks before Dinner*. That the major "character" in the play is named Edgar signals a departure for Doctorow from the strictly nonautobiographical work of which his oeuvre had previously consisted. For the two works that follow *Drinks before Dinner* and *Loon Lake* are also provocatively "autobiographical" and, taken together, *Drinks before Dinner*, *Lives of the Poets* (an equally experimental work), and *World's Fair* form a new phase in Doctorow's impressively versatile career. For a writer who had not created a typical early autobiographical novel because his strength "was *not* autobiographical writing" (*EC*, 34), this new phase has both personal and aesthetic implications that may well shape Doctorow's future artistic directions and development.

"A Theatre of Ideas"

Drinks before Dinner is Doctorow's first (and so far, only) experiment with the dramatic form and is, if we accept his explanation, a conscious attempt to create a theatrical mode that avoids the exhausted assumptions of "domestic biography" (xiv) that he claims are ubiquitous in contemporary theatre and television. These assumptions, Doctorow argues in the play's introduction, are a product of "sociological realism" and are distinctly at odds with the great forms of theater—"classical, absurdist, metaphysical, epic" (xiv). Implying that his own play will reflect one of these superior modes because it eschews the trappings of "sociological realism," Doctorow describes his effort as one that originated from a "sense of heightened language" (xi)—as opposed to character—and focuses on ideas: "I must here confess to a disposition for a theatre of language, in which the contemplation of this man's fate or that woman's is illuminated by poetry or philosophical paradox or rhetoric or wit. A theatre of ideas is what has always interested me" (xiii).

The play itself fully embodies this notion. Doctorow's caution to "future directors and actors of the play" (xviii) reinforces the flat, abstract, anti-realistic effects he hopes to achieve: "The actors should be discouraged from imagining histories for their characters or inventing relationships not indicated in the text. They should put on the words, as their costumes, and see what happens" (xix). The setting of the play, a "modern, well-appointed sitting room of a New York City apartment," and the characters themselves—three well-educated, upper middle-class couples, two typical middle-class children, a woman "artiste," and an important personage, probably representing the Secretary of State—are all (with the exception of Edgar) stereotypical and represent "the corruption of human identity" and "images of replicating humanity" (xv), which is the thesis of the play.

Edgar, the protagonist (and antihero who Doctorow calls "insufferable" [xvii]), is the only character who seems to recognize the paucity of their collective lives and his diatribes and jeremiads provoke the others into revealing their self-justifications, biases, and uncertainties. In addition to heightened dialogue, the only conventional "actions" of the play occur when Edgar quietly removes a gun from his pocket at the end of act 1, scene 1, and when Act 2 opens, Alan, the "guest of honor" and famous bureaucrat ("a recipient of the Nobel Prize for Peace" [38]), is tied to a chair with Edgar holding him at gunpoint. (Even the action of subduing Alan has taken place out of the view of the audience—presumably another of Doctorow's attempts to remove any vestiges of melodrama from the play.)

Stripped of every convention we have come to expect from theatre, *Drinks before Dinner* must, of course, engage its audience almost exclusively with the ideas debated in its "incantatory" (xviii) rhetoric. The burden thus shifts to Edgar and to the vision he espouses and forcefully debates with the other players, particularly Alan. For Edgar is "inconsolable" and believes that his and his friends' lives are empty, bereft of emotional content and moral purpose, essentially interchangeable—a theme that has steadily evolved in Doctorow's work from *Ragtime* to *Loon Lake* to this play (and will appear again in *Lives of the Poets*).

Once again exploiting the familiar metaphor of the automobile—originally introduced so forcefully in *Ragtime* with the Model T Ford and the dehumanizing assembly line that produced it—Edgar amusingly describes the mechanical nature of American lives and the endless repetitions of empty experience that are embodied in the frenetic, often pointless, driving of our ubiquitous cars (a metaphor used so effectively by Joan Didion in *Play It as It Lays*): "We have our life in cars" (18). Symbolizing death-in-life, the car (a "foreign car to express alienation" [21]) is the natural place from which—without premeditation or apparent purpose—Edgar buys the gun from a hoodlum who simply appears "standing at the driver's window" (22). And although we do not believe Edgar is likely to use the gun at this dinner party, the only active tension in the play—other than that engendered by the dialogue—is the remote possibility that he may, for: "Guns belong to the inconsolable. . . . But if you isolate me because I am holding this gun, if you decide I am on the brink of madness, for example, or over the brink, that could be ruinous" (23–24).

Outraged at being restrained and held at gunpoint, Alan assumes that he must begin the process of negotiation he would carry out with any common terrorist, and attempts a series of ploys to talk Edgar out of his notion (suggested by one of the terrified children) that the world is coming to an end, an assumption that is used by various fanatics to justify anarchistic acts of violence. But Edgar's sense of the world's ending has more to do with his painful (and for him, metaphysical) conclusion that the duplication of our lives; the "industrialization of our being" (39) has wiped out human character and the ability to make moral judgments or to have transcendent experience: "Anger is simply anger. Conflict is simply conflict. We are not elevated by it, nor do we learn from it, nor can we avoid repeating it" (41).

Although Alan recognizes some truth in Edgar's notion of the mechanical and depersonalized nature of modern life ("I have always felt my own character to be a fictional creation" [43]), his vision of "the end of the world" is ultimately wholly cynical, for he projects a "conspiracy of survivors" who would be "scientists and military men with government technology at their disposal" (49) plotting a sophisticated plan to ensure the survival of the fittest: "Only champions would be chosen, champions of survival, champions of selfishness, cunning, muscular strength, sexual vigor, children with the ability to kill, and a complete lack of concern for the horrors of their own consciousness" (49) who would be spirited away to a modern version of the ark, "some completely self-sustaining ecosystem . . . where the selected specimens of humanity can begin again" (49).

Horrified by Alan's prediction and by his shocking lack of idealism, the rest of the guests at the dinner party come to recognize that Edgar's vision—however bleak—implicitly holds out the possibility for a new beginning, and not the ceaseless repetition of the doomed past. Michael, one of the two characters who has some insight (the other being Andrea), repudiates Alan's view and begins to recognize the value of Edgar's position: "Edgar here sustains hope! All his despair for the way things are assumes there is something more. Everything he says expresses a longing for something more. Don't you, in your position, have the responsibility to want more—more than anyone?" (45).

Becoming increasingly cognizant of the horrible irony that Alan's apocalyptic prediction represents, Edgar summarizes the Secretary's cynical views in the incantatory prose of a modern prophet or choric voice and points the unloaded gun at the floor, squeezing the trigger and releasing all of the guests from their fear of his intentions. Now in character, Alan stalks out, delivering a diatribe of his own at Edgar, whom he characterizes as a "hypocrite of privilege," a "traitorous malcontent," a "spiritual vandal who would like to be a revolutionary but hasn't the balls of a flea" (51–52), and threatening some nefarious revenge for the "little entertainment" Edgar has devised. Having inadvertently galvanized the rest of the guests to share, at least to some extent, Edgar's vision, Alan leaves them to the incredible conclusion that they should simply "go in to dinner" (52). As Doctorow describes it, "a community of perception has been formed" (xviii).

Although as contemporary drawing-room drama *Drinks before Dinner* attempts some novel effects, it ultimately suffers far more mortally than *Waiting for Godot* from the problems inherent in the imitative fallacy, a fallacy that even the playwright acknowledges, only to defend: "So my characters are formal expressions of the basic passion of the play—an imitative fallacy perhaps, but only if you want from the theatre what you're used to" (xv). That it is nonetheless clearly a thesis play and that the thesis is the loss of human identity in no way frees Doctorow from the burden of creating interesting drama. Even if we grant him his donnée—his desire to create a "play turned inside out" (xvii)—the "contingency of the song" (xi), which he sees as the locus of the drama, must be extraordinarily compelling if the play is to be effective. What is so curious about *Drinks before Dinner*, therefore, is its failure to bring language dramatically alive, a skill Doctorow repeatedly displays in his fiction. Michael Feingold's assessment is, therefore, both perceptive and fair: "As a novelist, Doctorow has been able to invent ferociously dramatic scenes. . . . It seems puzzling that in most of *Drinks before Dinner* his writing is flat, prosy, and empty, lacking not only the curves of human speech but the sting of his own narrative style. . . . I salute his desire to say something gigantic; how I wish he had found a way to say it fully and dramatically."[3]

"Memories and Mousehairs"

While *Drinks before Dinner* was neither a commercial nor a critical success, it did introduce a character whose relationship to Doctorow seems more direct than any he had created heretofore in his fiction. Although he will not always name him Edgar, analogous or distinctly related characters appear in both *Lives of the Poets* and *World's Fair*. It is as if approaching and passing his fiftieth year, Doctorow chose—either consciously or unconsciously—to abandon many of the masks he had previously created in order to explore more directly his personal experience: the puppeteer, the ventriloquist, has ventured from behind the curtain. It would be a mistake, however, to assume that either Edgar or the writer Jonathan in *Lives of the Poets* is a simple surrogate for Doctorow. He has admitted that he used his own "memory as a resource" in writing *Lives* and *World's Fair*, but Doctorow has also denied that any of his recent characters are therefore autobiographical.[4] He has, in fact, always insisted upon his need to distance himself from his work. In 1980, speaking about the stark objectivity of *Welcome to Hard Times*, he made perhaps his clearest statement: "Somehow I was the kind of writer who had to put myself through prisms to find the right light—I had to filter myself from my imagination in order to write" (*EC*, 34).

What becomes apparent from a close study of *Lives of the Poets* is that its simple surface and ostensible structure are deceptive. Just as we must read the obviously complex *Loon Lake* more than once, we must also reread *Lives*, for which Doctorow has designed an analogous structure. Just as we cannot fully apprehend either the nature or the implications of Joseph Paterson Bennett's narrative until the final page of the novel, we cannot grasp the significance of the six stories in *Lives of the Poets* until we have read the revealing novella of the title. In both of these works—vastly different though they are—Doctorow has created nonlinear, spatial, virtually circular, structures. For without understanding that Jonathan—the whining, insecure, often insufferable (like Edgar in *Drinks before Dinner*) writer in the novella—is the author of the six stories that precede his confessional "I" narrative, the full power, form, and meaning of the work cannot be perceived. What at first seem in their linear arrangement to be a series of disconnected, sometimes interesting, sometimes confusing, mood pieces and psychological sketches take on entirely different colorations and significance when they are seen as the various fictional efforts of the man and artist Jonathan: "the pattern becomes meaningful when we encounter in the novella the voice of the author of the first six stories. Only when we have finished the book can we see all the connections. Then we are ready to read the stories again with a new understanding."[5] So what appears to be a collection of only vaguely related pieces may be read as a spatially constructed novel of sorts, even more radically fragmented than *Loon Lake*—a far cry indeed from what James Wolcott dismissed as "a shelf display of memories and mousehairs and glum, musing asides."[6]

There has rarely been a wittier, more mockingly self-reflexive and self-parodying portrait of the middle-aged artist than the narrator of *Lives of the Poets*, Doctorow's comic alter ego. Jonathan is a fifty-year-old, Jewish, relatively successful writer living tentatively in an apartment in Greenwich Village where he claims he has the necessary freedom and isolation to write. Although he worries maddeningly about petty physical annoyances from sore thumbs to scratchy throats to imagined bumps on his scrotum, he has stopped smoking, eats well, gets appropriate exercise, and has enough money to live comfortably, support several households, and travel whenever he wishes. Continually arguing with his estranged but "quick-witted and attractive" wife, Angel, he nevertheless visits her and their four children at their suburban home in Connecticut where "everyone in these woods is a writer" (121). He worries about his potency both as a male and as an artist, embraces fashionable leftist causes from saving whales to appearing at a "nuclear freeze poetry reading" (109), considers chic cure-alls for both physical and spiritual problems, attends dinner parties with the New York culturati, spends much time riding subways and otherwise studying the teeming city (particularly its many immigrants), indulges in repeated misogynistic judgments and perceptions (although he believes he is liberated), and is having an affair with a young woman Ph.D. and professor of literature ("an appalling profession" [127]) who is currently traveling in romantic and distant places from which she sends sentimental, sometimes cryptic, and ultimately devastating, postcards. He is Doctorow's archetypal contemporary artist and urban mensch, a wholly predictable, simultaneously annoying and amusing self-caricature reminiscent of any number of similarly self-reflexive Philip Roth, Saul Bellow, and Bernard Malamud characters.

Invoking Dr. Johnson's deadly serious *Lives of the Poets* (1779–81) for savagely ironic purposes, Doctorow clearly wants us to see the world of the contemporary artist as narcissistic, frequently shallow, and, more often than not, nonproductive. All the artist couples Jonathan knows are virtually mirror images of all the others: multiple marriages and affairs, flights and escapes into one panacea or sect or another, endless self-indulgence. They are, as Edgar would have it, interchangeable: the Pauls and Brigittes, the Mattinglys and Marikos, the Ralphs and Rachels, and all the other ethnically and religiously mixed and mismatched parodies of the contemporary cult of the aesthetic. Indeed, Doctorow gets even closer to the real New York literary scene with a mini-roman à clef staged at a publication party at the historic Dakota apartment house on Central Park West. For now the list has names we are meant to recognize: "Every writer who's in town is there, Norman and Kurt, Joyce, . . . I wave to Phil, there's Bernie, John, John A., Peter and Maria in from the Island." (141).

Even Jonathan's dreams and prayers for himself are predictable clichés: "Dear God, keep the blessings flowing, grant us all great good health and long life, with no illness, no sickness, no disease" (103) in a world where "you get to live and write a minimum hundred and fifty years, give or take a decade, and the cock never fails you" (82). Jonathan represents a specific literary and urban type of contemporary American everyman: alternately arrogant and insecure, guilt-ridden and self-indulgent, insensitive and romantic, socially committed and isolated, hopeful and despairing, materially comfortable and ascetic, he is symbolic of the artist testing both his life and his literary vocation. But he is *not* finally, simply Doctorow: "In creating the fictional Jonathan, Doctorow creates the fiction that he has made art out of his life; the truth is, he has created a life to account for the fiction."[7]

"A Life to Account for the Fiction"

In *Lives of the Poets*—and in another way in *World's Fair*—Doctorow creates a persona whose musings, fears, guilts, aspirations, sensibility, and experience are imaginatively transformed and distanced as they are shaped into the stories he writes. The six stories we read first are objectifications, in aesthetic form, of aspects of the quite flawed and very human character we finally come to know in the novella. By a process of induction, then, Doctorow creates Jonathan: "we're increasingly absorbed in understanding how the art-

ist revisits inhibiting, often traumatic experiences and reshapes them into objects that offer at least illusions of satisfactory completeness and control."[8]

Because "he says nothing directly about the process of writing fiction," but
rather "shows us how a writer's mind works,"[9] Doctorow's method is
oblique; he develops the relationships between the artist and his work in the
imagery of the stories, in their themes and tone, and we, as readers, partici-
pate by linking those components of the stories to the more conscious obsessions and monologue that is the novella. What is created, then, is created
totally by indirection, through spatial relationships that cut across the linear
and sequential arrangements of the linguistic structure; another form of
Doctorow's "printed circuit" is the result. *Lives of the Poets* can be perceived as
a unified structure, therefore, *only* when we understand that the amalgamat-
ing principle that fuses the disparate parts is Jonathan's fertile imagination.

"She Is Very Regal-Looking, My Mother"

Beginning the short-story sequence with the most fundamental of
relationships—that of a boy to his family, and, more specifically of Jonathan
to his family—Doctorow creates a structural and thematic framework for
Lives (he begins and ends with Jonathan). In so doing, he establishes—in its
immature manifestation—the life and mind of the incipient artist.

The story itself is simple and eloquent, for it reveals in just a few broad
brushstrokes the financially and emotionally stressed lives of a typical urban,
ethnic family during the 1950s wherein the American Dream of "the great
journey . . . from the working class to the professional class" (4) has failed to
materialize and the talented, but unsuccessful father, Jack, who has just died,
is blamed for "a pattern of business failures and missed opportunities" (8). In
addition to the normal pressures of premature death and financial hardship,
the family is also manipulated by Jack's wealthy and elitist aunts to invent a
lie about Jack's whereabouts in order to conceal his death from his "ancient
mother" and to provide her with the illusion that he has moved to Arizona,
where he is leading a financially rewarding and exciting life. Because he is the
"writer in the family," Jonathan is chosen to compose bogus letters to his
grandmother, which he does with more success than he can ultimately bear.

Discovering through the letter-writing charade that his father may indeed
have been both a reader and a dreamer much as he is, Jonathan blames himself for not having understood "while he was alive what my father's dream for
his life had been" (17). The story hereby establishes not only Jonathan's budding artistic talent and imagination, but it also demonstrates the root causes
of his lifelong affection for his misunderstood father and his profoundly

ambivalent feelings toward his "regal-looking" mother, who, on his fiftieth birthday portrayed in the novella, admits that she was at least partially responsible for his father's unfulfilled life: "He was a wonderful man, he had a fine mind. He did not think like anyone else. I didn't understand that, I tried to make him like everyone else" (*Lives*, 115).

Guilt about his relationship to both of his parents haunts the mature Jonathan. Remembering that when he was "maybe thirteen" he was manipulated by both of them and driven to take sides in their frequent conflicts, he acknowledges the ambivalence of his responses: "I would wake up to these terrible sounds of struggle, blows, cries, I didn't know whom to believe, whom to love, whom to defend, whom to attack, I felt this sick pleasure not knowing what I felt, hearing these sounds" (115). That these exceedingly painful memories of boyhood trauma remain vividly a part of Jonathan's imaginative life is made abundantly clear in the classically Oedipal story "Willi."

Placing the story in Galicia in 1910, Jonathan the writer escapes any overt connection between himself and the events that take place, except as they are part of his cultural heritage. For the family in the story is Jewish and has escaped its origins in "the alleys of cosmopolitan eastern Europe, like Darwin's amphibians from the sea" (32) to create an isolated, but extraordinarily successful, farm life. The tale is told by an adult male about a traumatic event that occurred when he was thirteen, the year "in the calendar of traditional Judaism . . . a boy enjoys his initiation into manhood" (31).

The event that precipitates a very painful initiation into manhood for Willi occurs when he accidentally observes his young and beautiful mother flagrante delicto with the equally youthful Christian tutor who is the only other human being with whom the family has regular contact. The boy is stunned and outraged: "I felt monstrously betrayed. . . . I wanted to kill him, this killer of my mother. . . . I wanted him to be killing her for me. I wanted to be him" (29).

Unable to force the betrayal from his mind, and alternately furious and sexually aroused by the images of his mother's ecstasy, he decides he must tell his father, a powerful, domineering individualist, twice his mother's age, whom Willi believes is "the god-eye in the kingdom, the intelligence that brought order and gave everything its value" (32). Communicating the terrible truth to his formidable father, Willi is nevertheless quickly brought to anguish when he realizes what his mother's fate will be. Hearing "the shocking exciting sounds of her undoing," he "sat up in bed, hardly able to breathe, terrified, but feeling undeniable arousal. Give it to her, I muttered, . . . But then I could bear it no longer and ran into their room and stood between them, lifting my screaming mother from the bed, hold-ing her in my arms, shouting at my father to stop, to stop. . . . I pushed her back and jumped at him, pummeling him, shouting that I would kill him" (35). The connection to Jonathan is clear. The story is an objectified expres-sion of the paradox he has personally experienced when he remembers the "terrible sounds of struggle" and feeling the "sick pleasure not knowing what I felt" (115). Like Willi, who assumes "I was the agency of his down-fall" (33), Jonathan subconsciously feels the predictable guilt of all chil-dren who believe they have somehow betrayed their parents, have somehow precipitated broken marriages and the destruction of adult lives. The dif-ference between Jonathan and the rest of us, Doctorow seems to be imply-ing, is that he has the potential to transcend traumatic experience and to achieve moral insight through his art. Ironically, this is the very virtue Jonathan attributes to his mother: "She is a good storyteller. She thinks narratively and comes to judgment through stories" (118).

Other Voices, Other Rooms

While we have examined in some detail two of the most powerful stories in the book in order to explore Doctorow's oblique method and subtle effects, the same kind of analysis is possible, although perhaps to a lesser extent, with each of the other stories. "The Hunter," for example, probably derives the in-tensity of its haunting images of isolation and undifferentiated anxiety from Jonathan's oscillating feelings of protectiveness toward and outrage against his mistress, "the Dark Lady of [his] sonnets" (93)—or alternatively, when she abandons him, "CIA cunt" (137).

It is a skillfully rendered story of the inexorable movement of an ideal-istic young woman's psyche from natural anxiety and loneliness to a self-paralyzing paranoia where inner and outer reality—fiction and truth—are indistinguishable from each other; a favorite Doctorow theme. The story also as a rare example in Doctorow's oeuvre of experience rendered from a woman's point of view—a woman who could be the imagined younger ver-sion of the emotionally peripatetic professor of English with whom Jonathan believes he is in love—is another potentially revealing artistic ex-pression of Jonathan's personal obsessions.

The remaining three stories in *Lives of the Poets* are less effective pieces than the three we have discussed so far. But each of them reverberates in one way or another with echoes of Jonathan's real or imagined life. "The Water Works" and "The Leather Man," for example, are really fragments, and each has a mysterious narrator who seems to be some sort of police or government official surreptitiously spying on the suffering or pain of others, sometimes, as in "The Water Works," with vicarious sympathy, but usually to identify and isolate those who are outsiders and nonconformists—the "derelicts" of society. That Jonathan is obsessively drawn to scenes of undercover police work commencing with his apartment window, and that he despises what he perceives as "the double life of state agencies, cops as cabdrivers, cops as bag ladies" and calls such activity "tribal theater" (128), probably helps explain his fascination with these characters and their shadowy, largely malignant presences in his stories. The CIA is, of course, his consummate target and, hearing a story from one of his cuckolded friends who makes a paranoid leap from seeing an unnecessary diaphragm in his wife's purse to assuming "Abigail was CIA" (129), Jonathan tells us how important that notion is to his perception of the world: "To discover your wife fucking someone else is one thing, but to be betrayed by the United States government is quite another. Think of it as a metaphor and it will begin to work for you as it has worked for me" (129–30). The less-than-successful stories that result from Jonathan's perceptions in this regard perhaps reveal his inability to place this particular obsession under the artistic control that he is able to manage so effectively elsewhere.

"The Foreign Legation" is a story that connects in several ways directly to Jonathan's current experiences. It details the empty life of a recently divorced man named Morgan, who, like Macon in Anne Tyler's *The Accidental Tourist*, is simply waiting for something, anything, to happen to change his now meaningless life.

What is particularly interesting about this story is how clearly Morgan is both a composite of all the deficient men with whom Jonathan is acquainted and a projection of what Jonathan himself could easily become, a victim of: "the lapse into dereliction" (122). "Dereliction is the state of mind given to middle-aged men alone, not to women" (101). And dereliction is a central motif in *Lives of the Poets*, for it links Jonathan's fear of his possible personal status as derelict ("I see the small spaces men end up with for their lives, and there is terror" [122]) and his sense of the necessary isolation of the artist: "between the artist and simple dereliction there is a very thin line, I know that" (101).

"Seek Transfiguration"

What Doctorow is ultimately attempting to achieve in *Lives of the Poets* is the simultaneous experience of a fictional writer's conscious—very human and often limited—mind, and the transmuted objects of that mind as it submits itself to the discipline and the magic of the creative process. We see the sometimes petty, egotistical man and we see the sometimes wonderful, sometimes ineffective, products of his imagination. But Doctorow has said the artistic is a metaphor for the personal and so, Jonathan quotes Rilke: "*Here there is no place that does not see you. You must change your life*" (138). While he struggles with his vocation as artist and is fearful that "I've become estranged from my calling" (131), he simultaneously struggles with his human identity and accepts Rilke's admonition that he must change his life.

Jonathan chooses to change his life in ways that are, finally, wholly predictable. Bullied by a sexy actress who was once his "hot muse" (138) and her "red-bearded rector in a clerical collar" (140), he makes a reluctant, but nevertheless personal, commitment to house an immigrant family of illegal aliens, probably from El Salvador.

By becoming personally engagé, Jonathan is, paradoxically, sacrificing the very freedom he believes is necessary to write; by becoming an active part of life, he may be renouncing the solitary artistic life, the reverse process that Doctorow has so effectively embodied in the experiences and choices of Joseph Paterson Bennett. But *Lives of the Poets* is fundamentally a hopeful book, and the concluding image of the novella suggests the potential for joining the artistic life to the active life. Sitting at his typewriter with the immigrant child on his lap, Jonathan grudgingly helps the boy to type: "each letter suddenly struck vvv he likes the v, hey who's writing this? every good boy needs a toy boat, maybe we'll go to the bottom of the page get my daily quota done come on, kid, you can do three more lousy lines" (145). Are they writing together what will become "The Water Works," a haunting story wherein a capsized toy boat comes to symbolize the drowned and pummeled body of an innocent young boy? In any case, Doctorow titillates us with the possibility of infinite interrelationships: " 'I found myself writing them in sequence as they appear in the book. As I read the stories over, I discovered a connection, like a mind looking for its own geography. I found that I was creating the character of the person creating them. So I wrote the novella to give him a voice. . . . To make something true, you have to use artifice.' "[10] And artifice will transfigure autobiography in *World's Fair*.

The Novelist as a Young Boy

World's Fair demonstrates yet again one of Doctorow's most attractive qualities, the refusal to repeat any of his previous fictional strategies, however successful. After the small, dark parable that is *Welcome to Hard Times*, after the flash and glamour of *Ragtime*, after the agonized electric shock of *The Book of Daniel*, after the rumble of energy that is *Loon Lake*, after the experimental self-reflexivity of *Drinks before Dinner* and *Lives of the Poets*, comes the quiet, finely textured *World's Fair*. It has, as we have suggested, most in common with *Lives*, especially "The Writer in the Family," and with the titular novella itself. The short story employs materials virtually identical with those of the novel while the novella suggests a distant projection of the novel's boy narrator into middle age and a career as a successful, if troubled, urban novelist. Numerous details of these stories are echoed in the novel.

We have previously noted the autobiographical elements in *Lives of the Poets*. Now, in *World's Fair*, after resisting the temptation to make his personal past essential to any of his previous novels—especially to his first, which in so many beginning writers hinges directly on the author's own life—Doctorow abandons himself fully to an account of his early childhood. Enough is known about the novelist's life from other sources, including his own interviews, to recognize that the line between the novel's materials and his own past experience is very difficult to distinguish. Doctorow has described his intention in *World's Fair* "to break down the distinction between formal fiction and the actual, palpable sense of life as it is lived."[11] The book, in fact, appears on the surface to be virtually a memoir recounted by a narrator with Doctorow's own first name, birth date, and biographical facts. Such an impression is reinforced by the reader's recollection of the appearance in earlier novels, especially *The Book of Daniel*, of some of the same details that are fully explored now: family life and family relationships, New York and the Bronx, ethnic culture, social and political landmarks.

There is irony and a charming audacity here, especially for a novelist who has often enough declared his rejection of realism—certainly the mode ostensibly adopted in this work—and a novelist who has also continually questioned the sanctity of historical fact. Having played fast and loose with history in book after book, having manipulated and distorted the recorded past and historical characters in order to achieve the kind of higher reality that he sought, Doctorow now records his personal history, with the intermittently seen larger world looming behind it, in what appears to be exquisitely accurate detail. We discover a careful delineation of "Edgar's" development against a background of very precise notations on geography, taste, economics, and social patterns; it is hardly surprising that some reviewers recommended the book to older New Yorkers on these grounds alone.[12]

Does Doctorow treat his own story as fiction because he has so consistently denied the validity (or insisted on the fictionality) of history? Is *World's Fair* to be seen as his own personal "false document"? He would argue, no doubt, that for the novelist, one's own history is just one more invented narrative.

Edgar's Book

At the very end of *World's Fair* Edgar tells how he and his friend Arnold, on a cold and windy day in October, buried their own time capsule in a corner of Claremont Park: "I think we both felt the importance of what we were doing," he remarks (371); so, we assume, does Doctorow, whose novel is itself a marvelously detailed time capsule. But whose time is recorded? The novel vividly recalls a small portion of geography and a much larger section of American experience. But Edgar Altschuler, the future writer, is Doctorow's invention of himself and the time chronicled is the boy's time—the first chapter in a Bronx bildungsroman.

World's Fair is the story of a boy born in 1931, two years after the American century turned sour; his narrative ends in 1939, just before the violent eruption that would permanently change the century. As the narrative proceeds, major events increasingly impinge upon, but are not allowed to displace, personal experience. Edgar's first report is the Joycean recollection of a very young child's bed-wetting and familial closeness, but most of the remaining account concerns the slightly older child.[13] His memories are in no sense disembodied or without clear context; his acute perception results in a story remarkably textured through rich detail and precise sense of location.

What he recounts, however, are the events that matter to him: the loss of the family dog, the arrival and unloading of a delivery of winter coal, buying hot sweet potatoes from the Sweet Potato Man, trips with his mother to the fish market, the shoe repairman, and the druggist, listening to radio programs, joining the family on their outing at Far Rockaway Beach, attending school and finding it to be the perfect arena in which to earn the applause he craves, schoolboy games, his affection for little Meg and their incipient sexuality (which is later reinforced by watching Meg's mother in a tacky side show act), watching the Hindenburg skim over New York, and then hearing of its fiery destruction, being set upon by knife-wielding toughs who call him "Jewboy" and threaten his life and, finally, late in the book, twice going to the World's Fair, first as the guest of Meg and her mother, then as a result of getting an honorable mention in an essay contest on the American boy.

Concomitantly and at a higher level of intensity, Edgar experiences the collapse of his mismatched parents' marriage and simultaneously feels the growth of his private life, discovers his grandmother dead in bed, witnesses the grisly death of a woman run down by a car, and nearly dies himself from a burst appendix.

Another "Little Criminal of Perception"

Given the concerns of Doctorow's previous fiction, it is not surprising to discover that the special perspective brought to bear on these experiences is that of the artist. Doctorow's emphasis here, however, is not on the moral sensibility of the mature and engaged writer but on the incipient artist's heightened perception—that primary faculty that, for Doctorow, remains the writer's essential priority, even after he develops the commitment to an examination of the world's wrongs. If, as Doctorow has claimed, this novel is in one sense about the struggles of children "to be moral beings," that morality demands of them a "very high-level perception"; they "must perceive, they must be almost engines of perception and judgment, in order to catch up to everyone else" (*DOP*, 197).

Edgar is, in fact, Daniel's "criminal of perception" at an early age. Given to "surveillance," a secret spy amid the lives of others (7), some of his first memories are of his compulsion to observe and note unseen. He records his detached study of his sleeping parents, seen as pure composition, concluding with the comment that "Together under the covers they made a pleasing shape" (5). He takes special delight in the color and texture of their slightly baroque bed and dresser: "I liked to lift each handle and let it fall back to hear the clink. I understood the illusion of the flowers, looking at them, believing them and then feeling the raised paint strokes with my fingertips" (5). He frequently exhibits the visual artist's appreciation of light, often combined with color and texture; when the city water truck sprays the streets, he is delighted: "Oh what a sight! An iridescent rainbow moved like a phantom light through the air, disintegrating as millions of liquid drops of sun and forming an instant torrent in the gutters at the curbstones" (24). He delights in his father's word games and his mother's metaphors, learns to read with magical ease, comes to value the "element of performance" (84) in his own response to life, and increasingly recognizes the importance and power of tricks and illusion. A circus clown's high wire performance is thus critical to his education and leads him to conclude:

There was art in the thing, the power of illusion, the mightier power of the reality behind it. What was first true was then false, a man was born from himself. All the problems of my own being were not the truth of me, I knew. . . . You didn't have to broadcast everything you knew all at once, but could reveal it suspensefully, and make them first cry out in fear, and make them laugh, and, above all, make them applaud, when they finally saw what an achievement had been yours by taking on so well and accurately the comic being of a little kid. (147)

It would be well for the reader of any Doctorow novel to note Edgar's obser-vation on the "power of illusion," and the last part of his statement suggests not only the budding novelist generally but, more specifically, the self-aware and self-ironical author of a novel like *World's Fair*. Finally, one of the boy's convictions about knowledge applies directly to our attitude to-ward Doctorow's art: "Truth hovered above everything waiting to alight, and as I grew older I saw that it never did anywhere, for any length of time" (97). Such, we have seen, is also the hard-earned wisdom of Blue and Daniel.

"Ventriloquism Self-Taught"

As the last quoted passages clearly demonstrate, the narrator's voice, whatever his perceptions, cannot be attributed simply to the boy whose story this is. Even literal autobiography is an act of invention; fictional autobiogra-phy grants, or demands, still more creative scope. Doctorow has created a narrator reminiscent of the one Joyce employs in his famous story "Araby." On one hand, the story and the narrator's reactions to it are supposed to be those of a young boy; on the other hand, the language and perspective are those of a mature and sensitive adult.

This conflation is reinforced by the boy's early awareness of his own pecu-liar position—"In my own consciousness I was not a child"—and in his pref-erence for solitary experience—"When I was alone . . . I had the opportunity to be the aware sentient being I knew myself to be" (22). At the same time, the boy details the problems of coming to grips with what he calls (in his adult voice) "the chaos of adult civilization" (144) and recognizes that, while he assumes "the comic being of a little kid," all is not simply performance: "I aspired to the power of myself" (147). He experiences, however, the classic agonies of childhood; defining his relationship to his parents, making sense out of the first intuition of sexuality and—above all—developing a complex identity. Again and again he is baffled by certain aspects of the initiation, even while he comes to recognize his own acute powers.

In much of this self-invention, Doctorow manages to keep the reader poised between childish experience and sophisticated reportage. There are moments, however, when one may feel that the narrative voice not only seeks to find mature ways to evoke childhood but also actually reconstructs that childhood in light of later judgment. For example, this small boy had only to see the special treatment afforded important people at a football game in order to awaken a radical consciousness: "Something in their atti-tude appropriated the occasion. It was theirs. The team was theirs, the ballpark was theirs, and I, standing with my runny nose and muffled to invisibility . . . on the outside and waiting to get in . . . I was theirs too. I felt all this keenly and became angry. Someone jostled me and I pushed back with my elbow" (261).

Or, taken by his older brother Donald on a trip through the seamier reaches of the city and observing various manifestations of poverty firsthand, Edgar immediately understands its economic moral: "How could I not with these sights in my eyes understand the meaning of a business? It was not an obscure lesson" (269). And though he had worshipped Frank Buck, the famous animal trainer, for living a life "adventurous yet with ethical controls" (336), Edgar comes to see him as an exploitive, selfish, and elitist man, largely, it appears, because Buck speaks of his Malay assistants as "boys" (337). Edgar's moral precocity is, of course, possible, but the rhetoric of judgment is so reminiscent of the book's author that one has the uneasy feeling that on occasion ventriloquism replaces the creation of the double vision. It is worth noting that Edgar, having first placed his copy of *Ventriloquism Self-Taught* in his time capsule, snatches it back out again, although, as John Sutherland puts it, "his other childish things are ritually put away."[14] Coming at the very end of the novel, this gesture appears to be a typical Doctorow joke, an acknowledgment of one central aspect of the novelist's craft that more idealistic claims may wish to ignore.

"An Autobiographical Poem"

World's Fair consists of thirty-one chapters of first-person narration and seven strategically located monologues by three family members—four by Rose, the narrator's mother, two by his older brother, Donald, and one by his wealthy aunt Frances. These seven short memoirs supply additional details and different perspectives, but their primary function is to corroborate the recollections and judgments of the narrator. Their tone reminds one of what is now loosely called oral history;[15] colloquial and informal, they sound very much like what might be captured on a tape recorder when some older, uneasy, and not terribly articulate relative attempts to sketch in those aspects of the past that he or she finds significant. In their realism, these interpolated passages contrast interestingly with the sometimes more literary prose of the primary narrator. A striking example of such contrast occurs at the book's outset, which opens with Rose's first monologue and is immediately followed by Edgar's first words. Summing up her courtship with Edgar's father, Rose says: "Things were different then, you didn't meet someone and go out and go to bed with them one two three. People courted. Girls were innocent" (3).

Rose's bald sentences and tone of stubborn insistence on the ways of the past provide a sharp contrast with Edgar's words that immediately follow; his speech introduces a distinctive and very articulate voice, one that helps establish his future status as novelist: "Startled awake by the ammoniated mists, I am roused in one instant from glutinous sleep to grieving awareness; I have done it again" (4). Despite the rich possibilities in the juxtaposition of gritty, unliterary testimony with the complex double voice of the narrator, Doctorow uses these interpolated passages less and less frequently as the novel moves into its second half, giving the impression that he simply allowed the device to trail off rather than that he realized its potential.

The rather Joycean passage from which the last quotation was drawn—indeed, even the bed-wetting, demands that the reader recall *Portrait of the Artist as a Young Man*—suggests one example of certain ranges of tone and style that have not pleased all readers. Some reviewers have lamented what they see as lyric excess; others have objected to a more characteristic restraint, a mock solemn style that is at times not unlike that of *Ragtime*. It may be that Doctorow is not always successful here in either tendency, but he certainly attempts something complex—the simultaneous awareness of the bright and sensitive child and the subtle articulateness of the adult. The reader may sometimes feel that in trying too hard to achieve this double vision, he imitates rather than simulates the verbal responses of the boy seen by the man. But if the prose in *World's Fair* is not everywhere successful, its general competence and moments of excellence surely outweigh its weaknesses and we are grateful to him for his typical willingness to take risks. A single example of his sustained eloquence can be found in his lyrical essay on "The beach at Rockaway in 1936" (77–79), which registers and orders a perceptual sweep that begins with the most fundamental physical senses, rises through recognition of the Manichaean mysteries of human sexuality, and culminates in the boy's ecstatic sense of belonging: "All this astonishingly was; and I on my knees in my bodying perception, wordlessly primeval, at home, fearful, joyous" (79).

The entire experience of sea and sand, men and women, is one of the rare climactic moments in this otherwise very quiet novel, a quietness curiously unaffected by passages of impassioned prose; nowhere else is Doctorow's fiction as subdued as it is, for the most part, in *World's Fair*. The narrator's very Wordsworthian realization of the world's "unutterable life" in this passage, reminds us that the novel's single epigraph drawn from *The Prelude*—"A raree-show is here, / With children gathered round"—should have prepared us for a quieter, more individualistic, perhaps even more meditative book than *Daniel, Ragtime*, or *Loon Lake*. Wordsworth's full subtitle to *The Prelude*—"Growth of a Poet's Mind / An Autobiographical Poem"—suggests Doctorow's previous volume, *Lives of the Poets*, and underscores his new and extensive commitment to personal experience in both volumes. Like Wordsworth, Doctorow recognizes that the spots of time remembered are the sparks that kindle creative fire; remembering is creating and creating remembering.

"Concentric Circles"

While roughly chronological, *World's Fair* has some of the topical and spatial qualities of *Ragtime*. Metaphorically speaking, one can see the novel as a series of concentric circles, or as one circle constantly expanding. At the novel's center is the boy's emerging life, particularly his perceptual life. Around this center circles his immediate family and other relatives. Beyond the extended family lies the Bronx and all of New York. Surrounding the city is the economically and politically troubled yet curiously hopeful America of the 1930s. Beyond America, but coextensive with it, looms the larger world, especially the inexorable growth of European fascism. Shielded for awhile by the scope of his vision, Edgar increasingly confronts these worlds, all of which impinge upon and help establish the direction of his life without actually determining it; the crucial factor remains the autonomous force of nascent creativity.

From the earliest sense of his parents' "godlike odors, male, female" (5) to his realization of their "irreducibly opposed natures," the conflict between his parents "was probably the major chronic circumstance" of his life. "Their differences created a kind of magnetic field" for him in which he "swung this way or that according to the direction of the current" (16), an emotional vacillation we have seen at work in *Lives of the Poets*. Before his inevitable disenchantment, Edgar believed that his father "got to where he was by magic" (9). A man who disliked boundaries, David Altschuler loved whatever was new, ignored security, gambled and perhaps philandered: he "lived by nature as a sojourner" (12). In later years the older son Donald would describe him as an antifascist and a leftist obsessed with the Sacco and Vanzetti case. Without wishing to do so, the father fatally damages his marriage and loses his successful music business. Capable of deep love for his family, he nonetheless has a "wild streak" (283) that almost destroys it.

Rose, both in her own monologues and in Edgar's descriptions, emerges as a strong, intelligent woman who struggles against various restraints: her inlaws, ethnic customs, growing poverty, her husband's combination of nerve and weakness. She is the moral force and ethical center of the family, yet—as is so often the case—her discipline is as tactless and wounding to a boy like Edgar as it is fair and just; with right on her side she nonetheless appears the least attractive parent. Such tension recalls "The Writer in the Family" and "Lives of the Poets," and, in its Oedipal and metaphoric manifestation, "Willi." Edgar's brother, Donald, is from the outset Rose's firm disciple, while Edgar discovers a natural affinity with his father, even while he comes to recognize his failings; he, too, is a dreamer, a lover of language and its possibilities, a free spirit who admires magic.

In her monologues Rose twice tells Edgar that only in the wreckage of her family did she come to see that their "lives could have gone in an entirely different direction" (35, 68), echoing the mother's admission to Jonathan on his fiftieth birthday in *Lives of the Poets*. Eloping rather than choosing a marriage inside the ethnic community and family neighborhood, Rose and David went to live by the ocean and Rose loved the sense of freedom in the open sea and sky. In this instance, the circle contracts; they are pulled back to the Bronx by the force field of a coercive if supportive family and culture and Rose's marriage is affected by the power of David's strong and selfish mother.

Though David is the family's ostensible entrepreneur, he is strongly inclined toward his own father's socialism. It is Rose who wishes "to move up in the world" (14); working for the Jewish Welfare Board, she not only understands but identifies with the immigrants' "desire to make good in America" (31). It is perhaps this alignment, this acceptance of the major American myth of mobility and achievement, that endows Edgar's portrait of her with some unpleasant taint. When Edgar says that Rose "measured what we had and who we were against the fortunes and pretensions of our neighbors" (14), we detect a clear note of distaste and, despite the obvious differences, we think of Rochelle Isaacson's character, another strong mother of a "little criminal of perception," and of Jonathan's mother in *Lives of the Poets*, who wants to know why his fellow writers are on television and he is not.

The Jewish culture in both its secular and religious forms comes to dominate this family sphere. Edgar's paternal grandfather is a self-educated and avid socialist, a free thinker whose son shares his politics and distaste for religion. His maternal grandmother, who comes to live with the family, is deeply devout, but Edgar, untrained in religious practice, views her room "as a dark den of primitive rites and practices" (46). His fear of her is reinforced by her fits of madness—we are reminded of Daniel's grandmother—and by the strangeness of her language: "I knew the name of the other language: Jewish. It was for old people" (46). Edgar finds that Jewish holidays compare unfavorably in some respects with secular American ones, though he finds attending a Seder at his wealthy aunt's interesting. When elderly men in prayer

shawls start coming to the door of their apartment with tales of Jewish persecution at the hands of the "brownshirt heathen" (126) and requests for the
support of Palestine, even the very American Bronx begins to appear unsafe,
although Edgar has only a shadowy idea of the danger.

This ethnic world is complete in itself and yet is firmly linked to the larger
American community. These neighbors are mainly Roosevelt supporters and
partially assimilated former immigrants. Rose's appreciation of the American dream represents, perhaps, the family norm. But this world is altered
when it is penetrated by frightening "old men's whisperings" (128). Tragic
tales from Europe evoke insecurity; even a little boy who goes to a Hebrew
school in the Bronx must "live in endlessly concentric circles of danger, . . .
rippling out over the globe" (128); "Jewish death was spreading" (127).

These new dangers from without—Jews had been "assigned" the "life of
prey" (128)—elide with an intensification of Jewish religious experience
brought about by Edgar's maternal grandmother's death, and the boy develops "the distinct impression death was Jewish" (124). But more important,
the new dangers reinforce the particular configuration of secular Jewish life
represented by Edgar's father and grandfather: intellectualism, atheism, socialism. His grandfather "came of a generation of enlightened Jewish youth
who understood . . . that religion was a means of holding people in ignorance
and superstition and therefore submissive to impoverishment and want."
Edgar does not really understand these arguments, but they became the familiar backdrop of family thought until he "was comfortable with their senti-
ments and was finally able to identify him [his grandfather] as a critic of
prevalent beliefs." Most important, "He was in opposition" (92). If, as John
Clayton has argued, Doctorow's vision is that of "radical Jewish humanism"
(*EC*, 109–19), then he dramatizes here one of its sources.

Father and grandfather worry not only about the Spanish revolution and
the rise of fascism, closer to home there is the poll tax and the lynching of
southern blacks; thus "Even our revered Roosevelt" (165) can be questioned
and faulted for political failures. Nor are American problems simply human
failures; some are systemic. Edgar senses that "European culture took re-
vengeful root in the New World" (128), repeating a theory that disturbs
Freud in *Ragtime*, and he also senses that the "powers" of class (272) were
clearly in evidence.

Early in the novel, when a swastika appears on the family's garage door,
the largest circle around Edgar's life begins to emerge. These are the latter
years of the 1930s; Hitler, at first only a sinister name and then a voice shrieking over the radio, begins to haunt the child's thoughts. Closer to home he
discovers that the thousands of American Nazis at a rally "shouted and

screamed just as the Germans did when Hitler spoke" (252). German refu-
gees purchase the duplex in which the family lives (making bad landlords);
eventually it becomes clear that "a terrible war had begun" (248) and he records the fall of France and later the Netherlands. Eventually he is attacked
by two knife-wielding toughs who teeter on the edge of maiming or murder
but finally just steal his money and call him "Jewboy" (305): the "endlessly
concentric circles" have collapsed into one.

But having noted this, it is necessary to emphasize that *World's Fair* is
not primarily concerned with the momentous events of this larger circle. As
we have earlier asserted, the macrocosm impinges upon, but in no sense displaces, the microcosm. Even the potentially tragic attack by the two boys
must be seen as a constant condition, like a bad climate, "because Christian
boys were like this all over" (307). There is, in fact, another more traditional way of looking at the novel's structure. Seen as a linear process, it
conflates two broad movements: the movement from absolute innocence to
some limited experience and the movement from security and limitation to
vulnerability and freedom. These journeys are, of course, essential for both
boy and artist.

The World Is Fair

At long last, near the end of the novel, Edgar finally gets to the fair—
twice, in fact. His first visit is with his friend Meg, a small and lovely child
whose single mother and shabby apartment represent a level of survival one
step down from the boy's own genteel poverty. Norma, Meg's mother, lives
life on the free but perilous fringe, in quite the opposite of his own mother's
cultural trap; and for Edgar her "freedom made life more thrilling and more
dangerous" (347). The Great Depression is not over; she is forced to perform
in one of the fair's sideshow acts, a tawdry farce involving a bogus octopus
and several female assistants who, while struggling with its tentacles, are
eventually stripped and assaulted in their glass-walled tank. Edgar's response
to the performance is a mixture of distaste and nascent sexual excitement.
The identification of the fair with sexuality is always vaguely present in the
book because of the sexual implications of the fair's logo, which is used in the
chapter headings, the Trylon and Perisphere: "white spire, white globe, they
went together, they belonged together as some sort of partnership" (321).[16]
For Meg, however, he feels the buddings of a less ambiguous love.

Edgar also arrives as "artist" when he earns an honorable mention in an
essay contest on the typical American boy. He is thus permitted to take his
family to the fair and, in introducing them to the previously explored realm,

he changes places with his father (who points out that Edgar is not a typical boy) and not only pulls something out of his hat—his father's old trick—but also assumes the role of leader and adventurer in the world of the new and unknown. Both excursions are therefore structurally and symbolically important; as the novel's climax, they mark the initial coming of age of a precocious child, the small triumph of knowledge earned, and a new vision of adulthood acquired: "I knew everything now, the crucial secret, so carelessly vouchsafed. . . . I had worried before, all the time in this enormous effort to catch up to life, to find it, to feel it, comprehend it; but all I had to do was be in it and it would instruct me and give me everything I needed. As I fell asleep the fireworks went off over and over again like me pounding my own chest and sending my voice to the heavens that I was here" (348).

Exhibiting the kind of multiple ironies that Doctorow loves, the year 1939 summons up out of Flushing Meadow the great vision of American innocence and idealistic progress bravely projected into the future, but a future soon to be brought into real doubt. If the Disneyland of *Daniel* is a theme park showing where we think we have been, perhaps Edgar's World's Fair is a theme park showing where we hoped we were going. In each instance reality is distorted, in the first case by pop mythologization, in the second by our naive technological faith. Nineteen thirty-nine, after all, brought Hitler's invasion of Poland and the outbreak of the world's greatest collective conflict. Even the literal fair, by the time the Altschuler family attends, shows signs of wear and tear, and Edgar's father cannot help but comment on the way its much-touted time capsule ignores all problematic and non-WASP aspects of American life. But despite the reader's knowledge of the outcome of the 1930s, in the last third of the novel that grim reality is largely eclipsed by the World's Fair and its role in Edgar's life. His experience in the Futurama is especially liberating; the extraordinary diorama showing a future technological Eden has, for him, a momentary potential, despite its studied avoidance of the unresolved political and economic difficulties of the previous decade. The title of the book, then, clearly puns, for now, in the moment of ecstatic recognition of individual and collective potential, the world *is*, paradoxically, fair—however unfair might be the world of 1939 and the future it will spawn.

"Illusion of a Memoir"

In his discussions of the novelist's social obligations, Doctorow has on several occasions sympathized with the failed political novels of the 1930s. Although in *World's Fair* the details of that grimy decade are everywhere keenly observed and beautifully rendered from the perspective of a small, sensitive boy growing up in the Bronx, only the most determined social critic will wrench this novel into political statement. Doctorow's memory is too long and his conviction too great for him to turn such a childhood as this into sentimental romance, but innocence is innocence, and in this novel he resists the temptation to chart the ragged and crazy edges of life. Some readers have found the results of his retrospective to be oddly restrained or strangely cautious, assuming, perhaps, that the biting ironies of *Ragtime* or the harsh analysis of *Loon Lake* must be transferred to his depression childhood. But however responsible that era might have been in shaping Doctorow's own social convictions, the narrative remains that of the boy as artist, not of the writer as political radical. This fact is nicely symbolized in Edgar's complete and utter absorption into the twentieth-century "raree-show": "As the evening wore on I forgot everything but the World's Fair. I forgot everything that wasn't the Fair as if the Fair were all there was, as if going on rides and seeing the sights, with crowds of people around you and music in your head, were natural life" (338). His family, school, the Bronx—all recede before an act of imagination experienced by most children, but in his case it is raised to the ninth power, before a created reality recreated in his mind so compellingly that it displaces all of the detailed factuality of life.

It is thus not in the evocation of the social world, however precisely done, but in the peculiar authenticity of the boy's experienced life that the novel's very considerable success lies; Doctorow implies that great forces are at work, leaving the reader to draw the implications, but he prefers to savour the richness of personal experience. Jonathan, the writer-narrator of *Lives of the Poets*, feels that "each book has taken me further and further out so that the occasion itself is extenuated, no more than a weak distant signal from the home station, and even that may be fading" (*Lives*, 142). Doctorow may share that feeling.

Reviewed with interest but not always with enthusiasm, often praised only with reservation, Doctorow's fictionalization of autobiography has been seen by some critics as lacking in vital novelistic qualities.[17] Indeed, choosing such a mode was dangerous; narrative, plot, and characterization—if Doctorow was to remain true to his past—all must be muted, especially when contrasted with his earlier innovative, mythicized, and sometimes controversial fiction. Given the nature of his material and its treatment, much of the book—especially the first two-thirds—often feels more like a literal autobiography than a novel; and in one way or another most reviewers have asked, "how much of this is true?" Doctorow might well reply, echoing his response to similar questions concerning the historical authenticity of *Ragtime*, "everything is true, now." And despite the willingness to resist his own talent for fictional pyrotechnics, his creation here of a personal false document is nonetheless a major achievement. However relatively quiet and understated this "illusion of a memoir" (as Doctorow himself has called it) may be in contrast to his earlier fiction,[18] it is neither guarded nor cautious in its invention of his own spiritual past;[19] above all, it beautifully communicates "the sense of a consciousness breaking through its shell."[20] It is, moreover, a novel that affectionately and movingly affirms the transcendent power of everyday existence.

Afterword: Doctorow at Fifty-five

We are cognizant of the dangers inherent in extensive and premature examinations of contemporary writers: those who seem to loom so large at the moment may, with little warning, disappear into the background of a very crowded and constantly shifting literary scene, leaving one to contemplate, somewhat sheepishly, one's transient enthusiasms. This would seem to be especially the case with a writer who has achieved great general popularity, even though he has apparently been taken quite seriously (if not always approvingly) by reviewers and critics. But there is little risk, it seems to us, that the fiction of E. L. Doctorow will cease to demand or to warrant such attention any time soon. With six novels, a play, and a collection of short stories spread fairly evenly over the last twenty-nine years, Doctorow, winner of an American Book Award, will no doubt—since he has consistently experimented with new forms and themes in each successive book—continue his firmly established pattern of innovation and discovery. In addition, his fiction has provoked an ever-increasing body of assessment and analysis, which is at least some indication that he has made a place for himself among the important writers of his time. Even as this book goes to press, a new novel, *Billy Bathgate*, has been published—a novel that may even further enhance Doctorow's reputation.

Because modern fiction is continuously evolving, even while some of its best practitioners are revitalizing traditional forms, we do not base our judgment on the experimental elements in his work alone—however successful they may be. Rather, we believe that Doctorow is the kind of pragmatic writer whose sense of style—point of view, structure, and other technical devices—is determined largely by his need to articulate a rich and vigorously held vision of human experience—individual and collective. The result has been a remarkable range of fiction, from the nearly perfect little tour de force that is *Welcome to Hard Times* and the passionate, agonized portrait of *Daniel*, through the elegant surfaces of *Ragtime* and the narrational intricacies of *Loon Lake*, to the quiet and understated personal record of *World's Fair*.

These works reveal a vision resonant with moral authority and yet at the same time wholly exploratory, provisional. The larger issues of social concern present are never allowed to reduce the chaos and ambiguity of experience to some dogmatic pattern of hope; again and again Doctorow acknowledges and accepts the enigmas produced by the conflict of desire and realization. In this confrontation he only asks that the reader fully consider the testimony of the moral imagination, that he bear witness to the artist's fallible but honest search for truth amid the complexities of modern life and the vagaries of the universe—where self and society remain forever unreconciled.

Notes and References

Preface

1. *E. L. Doctorow: A Democracy of Perception,* ed. Herwig Friedl and Dieter Schulz (Essen: Die Blaue Eule, 1988), 192. All references to this "symposium with and on E. L. Doctorow" will hereafter be indicated in the text as *DOP* with page number following.

Chapter One

1. Prescott, *Newsweek,* 19 November 1984, 107.
2. All subsequent references to and quotations from Doctorow's works will be from the following editions: *Welcome to Hard Times* (1960; New York: Bantam Books, 1976); *Big as Life* (New York: Simon & Schuster, 1966); *The Book of Daniel* (1971; New York: Bantam Books, 1979); *Ragtime* (1975; New York: Bantam Books, 1976); *Drinks before Dinner* (New York, Random House, 1979); *Loon Lake* (1980; New York: Bantam Books, 1981); *Lives of the Poets* (New York: Random House, 1984); *World's Fair,* (New York: Ballantine Books, 1985).
3. Bruce Weber, "The Myth Maker: The Creative Mind of E. L. Doctorow," *New York Times Magazine,* 20 October 1985, 74.
4. *E. L. Doctorow: Essays and Conversations,* ed. Richard Trenner (Princeton: Ontario Review Press, 1983), 53. All references to this collection of interviews with and essays on and by Doctorow will hereafter be indicated in the text as *EC* with page number following.
5. "The Passion of Our Calling," *New York Times Book Review,* 25 August 1985, 21.
6. Ibid.
7. Ibid.
8. Roth, *Reading Myself and Others* (New York: Farrar, Straus & Giroux, 1975), 120.
9. "The Passion of Our Calling," 23.
10. Ibid.
11. Epstein, "A Conspiracy of Silence," *Harper's,* November 1977, 86. Epstein's article is echoed by others but remains the best example of this attitude toward Doctorow and other dissenting novelists. Trilling raised the issue of the artist as cultural adversary in *Beyond Culture* (New York: Viking Press, 1968). He generalizes on the subject in the preface, from page xiii of which our quotation is drawn.
12. Epstein, "A Conspiracy of Silence," 86, 80.
13. Ibid., 92.

14. Two examples are John Clayton's "Radical Jewish Humanism: The Vision of E. L. Doctorow" (*EC*, 109–19), and David S. Gross's "Tales of Obscene Power: Money and Culture, Modernism and History in the Fiction of E. L. Doctorow" (*EC*, 120–50). Both articles offer useful insight into Doctorow's work, despite their relentless political bias.

15. *Black Women Writers* (1950–1980), ed. Mari Evans (Garden City, N.Y.: Doubleday, 1984), 344.

16. "A Multiplicity of Witness: E. L. Doctorow Heidelberg," *DOP*, 188. His response on this occasion is all the more significant because it is directed at an audience of German intellectuals.

17. Victor S. Navasky, "E. L. Doctorow: 'I Saw a Sign'" (interview), *New York Times Book Review*, 28 September 1980, 44.

18. Cooke, *Acts of Inclusion* (New Haven, Conn.: Yale University Press, 1979), xi.

19. Kundera, *The Art of the Novel* (New York: Grove Press, 1988), 7.

20. George Plimpton, "The Art of Fiction: E. L. Doctorow," *Paris Review* 101 (1986):28.

21. Ibid., 29.

22. *EC*, 53. Several critics have illuminated the Jewish element in Doctorow; see John Clayton, "Radical Jewish Humanism" *EC*, 109–19; Mildred Culp, "Women and Tragic Destiny in Doctorow's *The Book of Daniel*," *Studies in American Jewish Literature* (1982):155–66; Robert Forrey, "Doctorow's *The Book of Daniel*: All in the Family," *Studies in American Jewish Literature* 2 (1982):167–73; Sam B. Girgus, "A True Radical History: E. L. Doctorow," *The New Covenant: Jewish Writers and the American Idea* (Chapel Hill: University of North Carolina Press, 1984), 160–83.

23. See Cooper, "The Artist as Historian in the Novels of E. L. Doctorow," *Emporia State Research Studies* 29, no. 2 (Fall 1980):4–44; Emblidge, "Marching Backward into the Future: Progress as Illusion in Doctorow's Novels," *Southwest Review* (1977):397–409; Friedl, "Power and Patterns of Historical Process in the Novels of E. L. Doctorow," *DOP*, 19–44.

24. "The Passion of Our Calling," 23.

Chapter Two

1. There are three different statements by Blue about the origin of the ledgers. The first indicates that Blue bought the ledgers from a lawyer "who had passed through a year before, dumping everything he owned so as to march on unencumbered up to the mining camp in the lodes" (23). Another ledger was apparently obtained from "a traveling notions man" (101). These original ledgers, with the exception of the covers, are burned in the first of Clay Turner's conflagrations in *Hard Times*. The origin of the ledgers we are presumably reading is much clearer:

"Alf had left me three ledgers and a steel-point pen to keep the Express accounts. But there was enough paper in the ledgers to write the Bible" (124).

2. Major Munn, an old veteran, refers to his courage at Richmond (21). Given his approximate age, it would seem the time is somewhere in the 1880s or 1890s. The Dakotas became states in 1889.

3. There has been a proliferation of the antiwestern since 1960, including two very recent efforts, both of which echo elements of Thomas Berger's *Little Big Man* (published in 1960, the same year as *Hard Times*) as well as Doctorow's novel: Greg Matthews's woefully despairing but riveting *Heart of the Country* (New York: W. W. Norton Co., 1985) takes Berger's theme one step closer to unrelenting, almost sadistic, nihilism, while Larry McMurtry's marvelous saga of the founding of the Montana territories, *Lonesome Dove* (New York: Simon & Schuster, 1985), features a talker and optimist, Augustus (Gus) McCrae, who is much like Blue in his belief in the civilizing forces of human settlement.

4. See, for example: J. Bakker, "E. L. Doctorow's *Welcome to Hard Times*: A Reconsideration," *Neophilologus* 69, no. 3 (1985):464–73; Marilyn Arnold, "History as Fate in E. L. Doctorow's Tale of a Western Town," *EC*, 207–16; and Gross, "Tales of Obscene Power," *EC*, 120–50.

5. Tanner, "Rage and Order in Doctorow's *Welcome to Hard Times*," *South Dakota Review* 22, no. 3 (1984):84.

6. Ibid., 83.

7. Ibid., 82.

8. For excellent discussions of the contrast between Doctorow's vision and the values implicit in these earlier "westerns" see J. Bakker, "The Western: Can It Be Great?" *Dutch Quarterly Review of Anglo-American Letters* 14, no. 2 (1984):140–63, as well as Bakker, "A Reconsideration."

9. In an interview with Jared Lubarsky, Doctorow clearly links creation and discovery: "You trust the act of writing. You let it discover what it is you're doing," "History and the Forms of Fiction," *Eiso Seinen. The Rising Generation* 124 (1978):150.

10. Doctorow repeatedly uses the image of the connecting circuit in both his essays and interviews, describing the transactional activity between writer and reader, but, perhaps most dramatically, in a variety of metaphoric ways in *The Book of Daniel*.

11. As Robert Towers remarks in his review of *Loon Lake*, "it is impossible to predict even roughly the shape, scope and tone of one of his novels from its predecessors" ("A Brilliant World of Mirrors," *New York Times Book Review*, 28 September 1980, 1).

12. Weber, "The Myth Maker," 42.

13. Navasky, "'I Saw a Sign,'" 44.

14. Levine, *E. L. Doctorow* (London and New York: Methuen, Contemporary Writers Series, 1985), 34.

15. Weber, "The Myth Maker," 42.

Chapter Three

1. Robert Meeropol and Michael Meeropol, *We Are Your Sons* (New York: Ballantine Books, 1975). In an interesting article Joseph W. Turner has classified *Daniel* as a "disguised" historical novel and believes that the novel cannot be read intelligently without reference to the Rosenberg case, see "The Kinds of Historical Fiction: An Essay in Definition and Methodology," *Genre* 12 (1979):347–48. We do not accept that conclusion.

2. Pearl K. Bell's almost perverse misreading is a case in point. Ignoring the critical nature of point of view in this novel—the way Doctorow has created what we have seen him call a "false document"—she finds the novel "unequivocally committed to a conspiratorial view" of the trial and execution and Doctorow filled with "didactic zeal to spell out these convictions" ("Singing the Same Old Songs," *Commentary* 70 [1980]:72. See also Epstein, "A Conspiracy of Silence," *Harper's* 255 (Nov. 1977):88, who acknowledges that the book is Daniel's but accuses Doctorow of an attempt to "rig his novel, in ways both little and large, for what can only be political purposes." At the other extreme are such statements as Paul Levine's: "*The Book of Daniel* is the best and most important American novel of the 1970's" (*EC*, 183).

3. Harpham, "E. L. Doctorow and the Technology of Narrative," *PMLA* 100, no. 1 (January 1985):83.

4. *EC*, 169. Sternlicht's New Left repudiation of American Communists parallels the generally negative view of the party in the novel, for instance the implication that it had abandoned the Isaacsons until their case offered propaganda value.

5. Sternlicht's significant trash reminds one of Donald Barthelme's dreck-as-art theory, especially in such stories as "See the Moon" and "Indian Uprising." One might also add that the main trope of Doctorow's *Big as Life* anticipates the sort of thing that Barthelme does in "The Balloon."

6. Dillard, *Living by Fiction* (New York: Harper and Row, 1982), 21.

7. This judgment is, in fact, very close to what seems to have happened in the Rosenberg trial, especially in the case of Ethel. See Ronald Radosh and Joyce Milton, *The Rosenberg File: A Search for the Truth* (New York: Holt, Rinehart and Winston, 1983), passim.

8. In discussions with Doctorow interviewers have implied and, in at least one place matter-of-factly stated that the "the Isaacsons are framed" (*ED*, 44). On these occasions Doctorow has allowed the assumption to stand, although his actual response always moves the discussion away from literal facts.

9. For example, see "Martyrdom and After," *TLS*, 18 February 1972, 173.

10. Charyn, *New York Times Book Review*, 4 July 1971, 6.

11. For the probable influence of revisionist historian William Appleman Williams on Doctorow's view of the cold war, see Daniel L. Zins, "Daniel's' Teacher' in Doctorow's *The Book of Daniel*," *NMAL* 3 (1979):item 16.

12. Girgus has called *Daniel* "one of the great Jewish novels of our times" ("A

True Radical History," 165). For discussion of the Jewish element in Doctorow, see Chapter 1, note 21.

13. Alter, "The American Political Novel," *New York Times Book Review*, 10 August 1980, 3.

14. This passage bears a remarkable similarity to Robert Lowell's description, in "Memories of West Street and Lepke" (*Life Studies* [London: Faber, 1968]), of another cold war witness who has undergone a similar withdrawal, Czar Lepke:

> Flabby, bald lobotomized,
> he drifted in a sheepish calm,
> where no agonizing reappraisal
> jarred his concentration on the electric chair—
> hanging like an oasis in his air / of lost connections
> (90)

One of Daniel's central motifs involves "connections," and the equation of personal psychological disturbance with public "sickness" is, of course, central to many of Lowell's poems and strongly operative in *The Book of Daniel*. The "agonizing reappraisal" had been the famous and, to many, ironic, statement by John Foster Dulles concerning America's nuclear deterrent, which is also relevant here.

15. The argument is most relentlessly made by Cooper in "The Artist as Historian."

16. Lorsch, "Doctorow's *The Book of Daniel* as Künstlerroman: The Politics of Art," *Papers in Language and Literature* 18 (1982):385.

17. Harpham, "Technology of Narrative," 87–88.

Chapter Four

1. The publication of *Ragtime*, the media campaign mounted on its behalf, its commercial success, and the critical reaction, compose a remarkably interesting subject, on both literary and cultural grounds. Among other discussions, see Eliot Fremont-Smith, "*Ragtime* Jackpot: How to Make a Million Bucks in Just One Day," *Village Voice*, 25 August 1975, 35–36; Greil Marcus, "*Ragtime* and *Nashville*: Failure-of-America Fad," *Village Voice*, 4 August 1975, 96, 61–62; John Sutherland, "The Selling of *Ragtime*: A Novel for Our Times?" *New Review* 4, nos. 39–40 (1977):3–11.

2. Larry McMurtry's comment is representative: "Probably no good book has been as oversold as *Ragtime*. Doctorow must recognize that he has been the beneficiary of a terrific hype" ("O Ragged Time Knit Up Thy Ravell'd Sleeve," *American Film* no. 2, 3 [December–January, 1977], 5).

3. Rodgers, "A Novelist's Revenge," *Chicago Review* 27 (1976):139.

4. Gardner, *Moral Fiction*, (New York: Basic Books, 1978), 78–79.

5. Lubarsky, "History and the Forms of Fiction," 60.

6. Responding to a comment on the cinematic element in his novels, Doctorow has said that he "does not know how anyone can write today without

accommodating eighty or ninety years of film technology," since modern readers have been so deeply influenced by that art form; "what we've learned from film is quite specific. We've learned that we don't have to explain things" (*EC*, 40–41). On the aesthetic, social, and economic relationship of film to *Ragtime*, see Anthony Dawson, "*Ragtime* and the Movies: The Aura of the Duplicable," *Mosaic: A Journal for the Interdisciplinary Study of Literature* 16, nos. 1–2 (1983):205–14; Angela Hague, "*Ragtime* and the Movies," *North Dakota Quarterly* 50, no. 3 (1983):101–12.

7. Hague sees "Doctorow's prose style, with its almost hypnotic repetition of short, standard English sentences which rarely make use of metaphorical or figurative language" as an "attempt to approximate the mysterious opacity of the photographed image. . . . It is as if the narrator presents the reader with an interminable series of photographs and challenges him to decipher them" ("*Ragtime* and the Movies," 110).

8. Grumbach, "A Last Hurrah," *New Republic*, 5 July 1975, 31.

9. Navasky, "E. L. Doctorow: 'I Saw a Sign,'" 44.

10. Walter Clemons, "Houdini, Meet Ferdinand," *Newsweek*, 14 July 1975, 76.

11. Mel Gussow, "Novelist Syncopates History in *Ragtime*," *New York Times*, 11 July 1975, 12.

12. "The Passion of Our Calling," 23.

13. In "The Passion of Our Calling" Doctorow, rejecting "esthetic piety," very clearly outlines the major distinction between the aesthetic view of literature typical in American culture and the ideological view of such world novelists as Nadine Gordimer and Günter Grass who, he believes, would find the American view "a source of amusement" (21, 22).

14. Clemons, "Houdini, Meet Ferdinand," 76.

15. Scholes, "Fabulation as History: Barth, Garcia-Marquez, Fowles, Pynchon, Coover," *Fabulation and Metafiction* (Urbana: University of Illinois Press, 1979), 206.

16. Coover, *The Public Burning* (New York: The Viking Press, 1977), 136.

17. Sale, "From Ragtime to Riches," *New York Times Review of Books*, 7 August 1975, 21.

18. Moses, "To Impose a Phrasing on History," *Nation*, 4 October 1975, 311.

19. Sale, "From Ragtime to Riches," 21.

20. Green, "Nostalgia Politics," *American Scholar* 45, (1975–76):842.

21. Marcus, "*Ragtime* and *Nashville*," 61.

22. Ibid., 62.

23. Ibid., 61.

24. Kramer, "Political Romance," *Commentary*, October 1975, 79.

25. Ibid., 78.

26. Eliot Fremont-Smith chooses to defend Doctorow from this attack by suggesting that Kramer is the kind of critic "who will find the cake where none exists,

where it's all, or very nearly all, icing—and who in the process is likely to miss how very wonderful really proper icing can be. Which is to say," he adds, that "*Ragtime* is what it is and not horrendously much of anything else: a most elegant, beautifully done . . . confection: a comedy." But surely this neither explains nor rescues the novel; aside from the unfortunate confectionery imagery, it reinforces the claim that *Ragtime* is all surface, a quality that we have seen Sale applaud but that most hostile critics have pointed to as a way of explaining the book's great popularity without having to grant it any merit. "Making Book," *Village Voice*, 17 November 1975, 55.

27. Levine, *E. L. Doctorow*, 9. Doctorow has several times acknowledged his debt to Hawthorne and the romance; see, for example, *DOP*, 194–95.

28. Evans, "Impersonal Dilemmas: The Collision of Modernist and Popular Traditions in Two Political Novels, *The Grapes of Wrath* and *Ragtime*," *South Atlantic Review* 52, no. 1 (January 1987):81. Girgus reminds us that like Nietzsche, Doctorow recognizes that history alone, without myth, becomes an empty abstraction ("A True Radical History," 161).

29. See pp. 132–35, 178, 301–302.

30. See pp. 76, 129, 131, 365.

31. Dawson, "*Ragtime* and the Movies," 208.

32. Pierce, "The Syncopated Voices of Doctorow's *Ragtime*," *Notes on Modern American Literature* 3 (1979):item 26.

33. Brienza, "Doctorow's *Ragtime*: Narrative as Silhouettes and Syncopation," *Dutch Quarterly Review of Anglo-American Letters* 2, no. 3 (1981):101.

34. Kriegel, "The Stuff of Fictional History," *Commonweal* 102, no. 20 (1975):632.

35. Todd, "The Most-Overrated-Book-of-the-Year Award, and Other Literary Prizes," *Atlantic Monthly* 237 (1976), 96.

36. Jeffrey Hart, "Doctorow Time," *National Review*, 15 August 1975, 893.

37. Doctorow has openly acknowledged his debt to Kleist several times. "When I first read Kleist I recognized a brother," he has said, having realized "the location of his narrative [to be] somewhere between history and fiction" (*DOP*, 194). A number of scholars have examined the details and significance of his borrowings; see for example Josie P. Campbell, "Coalhouse Walker and the Model T Ford: Legerdemain in *Ragtime*," *Journal of Popular Culture* 13 (1980):302–309; Robert E. Helbing, "E. L. Doctorow's *Ragtime*: Kleist Revisited," *Heinrich Von Kleist Studies* (New York: AMS Press, 1980), 157–67; Marion Faber, "Michael Kohlhaas in New York: Kleist and E. L. Doctorow's *Ragtime*," also in *Heinrich Von Kleist Studies*, 147–56.

38. James Lincoln Collier, "The Scott Joplin Rag," *New York Times Magazine*, 21 September 1975, 19.

39. Rodgers, "A Novelist's Revenge," 141.

40. Moses, "To Impose a Phrasing on History," 312.

Chapter Five

1. Towers, "A Brilliant World of Mirrors," *New York Times Book Review*, 28 September 1980, 47.

2. Ibid.

3. Bell, "Singing the Same Old Songs," *Commentary*, October 1980, 73.

4. As Margaret Atwood wryly suggests of *Loon Lake*, "It's a sad commentary on the state of publishing, . . . that if it weren't by the author of *Ragtime* most commercial publishers would have rejected it as too literary. That Doctorow's verbal acrobatics by no means exclude involvement suggests that the line between 'literature' and 'entertainment' is one drawn by publishers rather than writers" (*Second Words* [Boston: Beacon Press, 1980], 326).

5. Peter S. Prescott, "Doctorow's Daring Epic," *Newsweek*, 15 September 1980, 88.

6. Doctorow describes the novel as such in an interview with Larry McCaffery found in Tom LeClair and Larry McCaffery's *Anything Can Happen: Interviews with Contemporary American Novelists* (Urbana: University of Illinois Press, 1983), 99.

7. George Stade, "Types Defamiliarized," *Nation*, 27 September 1980, 285.

8. Libby, an innocent servant at Loon Lake, tells Joe that Bennett owns thirty thousand acres (73). Two other references in the novel suggest that the estate's size is fifty thousand acres (83, 282).

9. Flower, "Fiction Chronicle," *Hudson Review* (1981):106.

10. Curran, Review of *Loon Lake* in *World Literature Today* 55, no. 3 (1981):472.

11. Brownjohn, "Breaking the Rules," *Encounter* 56 (1981):86.

12. See Bell, "Singing the Same Old Song," 70, and Towers, "A Brilliant World of Mirrors," 46.

13. Curran, review of *Loon Lake*, 472.

14. E. L. Doctorow in an interview with Victor S. Navasky, "E. L. Doctorow: 'I Saw a Sign,'" 44.

15. LeClair and McCaffery interview in *Anything Can Happen*, 99.

16. Johnson, "The Righteous Artist: E. L. Doctorow," in *Terrorists and Novelists* (New York: Knopf, 1982), 144.

17. Levine, *E. L. Doctorow*, 74.

18. Stade, "Types Defamiliarized," 286.

19. Bell, "Singing the Same Old Songs," 72.

20. Harpham, "Technology of Narrative," 94–95.

21. See introductory notes to Conrad's work in *Ten Modern Masters*, ed. Robert Gorham Davies (New York: Harcourt, Brace and Company, 1953, 1959), 69–70.

22. Conrad, *Heart of Darkness*, Norton Critical Edition, ed. Robert Kimbrough (New York: W. W. Norton & Co., 1963), 79.

23. Ibid., 71.

24. If the submerged Conrad analogy seems to lack sufficient justification in

the text, we have only to recall the elaborate and equally buried use of Kleist in *Ragtime*. Both allusions are available to only a small minority of Doctorow's audience, yet both supply Doctorow with creative analogies helpful in realizing his story.

25. Harpham, "Technology of Narrative," 92.

26. Ibid., 93.

27. See Alan Nadel's essay in which he adds this perceptive caveat to Harpham's analysis, "Hero and Other in Doctorow's *Loon Lake*," *College Literature* 14, no. 2 (1987):142.

28. Ibid., 90.

29. Diane Johnson, "The Righteous Artist," 141–49.

30. Girgus, "A True Radical History," 181.

31. Johnson, 148.

32. Ibid., 148–49.

33. Ibid., 148.

34. Harpham, "Technology of Narrative," 93.

Chapter Six

1. Levine, *E. L. Doctorow*, 77.

2. See Random House edition for note on first production and introduction, xi–xx.

3. Feingold, "Not with a Bang," *Village Voice*, 4 December 1978, 121.

4. "The Art of Fiction," 30; see also *DOP*, 190.

5. Levine, *E. L. Doctorow*, 79.

6. James Wolcott, "Ragtime," *New Republic,* 3 December 1984, 31.

7. Prescott, "The Creative Muse," *Newsweek*, 19 November 1984, 107.

8. Bruce Allen, "It Was a Very Good Year: Doctorow's *Lives of the Poets*," *Christian Science Monitor*, 4 January 1985, B2.

9. Peter Prescott, "The Creative Muse," 107.

10. Herbert Mitgang, "Finding the Right Voice," *New York Times Book Review*, 11 November 1984, 42.

11. Weber, "The Myth Maker," 78.

12. E.g., Christopher Lehmann-Haupt, *New York Times*, 31 October 1985, C21.

13. In addition to Joyce, some readers will recall another Irish writer, Frank O'Connor, whose work, especially "My Oedipus Complex," offers a narrative voice that is similar to Edgar's.

14. Sutherland, "Edgar and Emma," *London Review of Books*, 20 February 1986, 18.

15. Doctorow has admitted that such was his intention. "The Art of Fiction," 27.

16. Mary C. Erler, *America*, 8 March 1986, 193.

17. David Leavitt, for example, in a thoughtful review, "Looking Back on the World of Tomorrow," argues that this "peculiar hybrid of novel and memoir" is only

fully successful in its final third. "Its structure is that of an autobiography . . . but where a work of biography derives its imperative from the significance of the life it describes, in a novel, it is the author, not the subject, who must provide the reader with a sense of what to read for"; the reader has a right to expect "an organizing principle more substantive than chronology" *New York Times Book Review*, 10 November 1985, 3–4).

18. Weber, "The Myth Maker," 78.

19. Both terms are used in a particularly imperceptive review by R. Z. Sheppard, "The Artist as a Very Young Critic," *Time*, 18 November 1985, 107.

20. Richard Eder, review of *World's Fair, Los Angeles Times*, 24 November 1985, B3.

Selected Bibliography

PRIMARY WORKS

Novels and Stories

Big as Life. New York: Simon & Schuster, 1966.
Billy Bathgate. New York: Random House, 1989.
The Book of Daniel. New York: Random House, 1971.
Lives of the Poets: Six Stories and a Novella. New York: Random House, 1984.
Loon Lake. New York: Random House, 1980.
Ragtime. New York: Random House, 1975.
Welcome to Hard Times. New York: Simon & Schuster, 1960.
World's Fair. New York: Random House, 1985.

Play

Drinks before Dinner: A Play. New York: Random House, 1979.

Other Works

"False Documents." *American Review* 26 (November 1977):215–32.
"Living in the House of Fiction." *Nation*, 23 April 1978, 459–61.
"The Passion of Our Calling." *New York Times Book Review*, 25 August 1985, 1, 21–23.
"The Beliefs of Writers." *Michigan Quarterly Review* 37 (Fall 1985):606–19.

SECONDARY WORKS

Books

Friedl, Herwig, and **Dieter Schulz,** ed. *E. L. Doctorow: A Democracy of Perception*. Essen: Die Blaue Eule, 1988. Very useful recent interview and essays from the European perspective.

Levine, Paul. *E. L. Doctorow*. London and New York: Methuen, 1985. Essential study, especially of Doctorow's social/political themes.

Trenner, Richard, comp. and ed. *E. L. Doctorow: Essays and Conversations*. Princeton: Ontario Review Press, 1983. Essential collection; includes two seminal essays by Doctorow, three interviews, and several important critical discussions.

Parts of Books, Articles, and Interviews

Arnold, Marilyn. "History as Fate in E. L. Doctorow's Tale of a Western Town." *South Dakota Review* 18 (1980):53–63. (Reprinted in Trenner, *Essays and Conversations*, 207–16.) An interesting study of the cyclical nature of history and its images in *Hard Times*.

Bakker, J. "The Western: Can It Be Great?" *Dutch Quarterly Review of Anglo-American Letters* 14, no. 2 (1984):140–63. Contrasts contemporary "westerns" such as *Hard Times* with earlier, more romantic, versions of the West.

Brienza, Susan. "Doctorow's *Ragtime*: Narrative as Silhouettes and Syncopation." *Dutch Quarterly Review of Anglo-American Letters* 2, no. 3 (1981): 97–103. Examines the spatial, temporal, and aural implications of Doctorow's narrative.

Clayton, John. "Radical Jewish Humanism: The Vision of E. L. Doctorow." *Fiction International* 10 (1977):60–64. (Reprinted in Trenner, *Essays and Conversations*, 109–11.) Useful, if militant, discussion of Doctorow's ethnic loyalties.

Cooper, Barbara. "The Artist as Historian in the Novels of E. L. Doctorow." *Emporia State Research Studies* 29, no. 2 (Fall 1980):5–44. Early and seminal study of Doctorow's uses of history.

Emblidge, David. "Marching Backward into the Future: Progress as Illusion in Doctorow's Novels." *Southwest Review* (1977):397–409. Excellent insight into Doctorow's existential vision.

Foley, Barbara. "From *U.S.A.* to *Ragtime*: Notes on the Forms of Historical Consciousness in Modern Fiction." *American Literature* 50, no. 1 (1978):85–105. (Reprinted in Trenner, *Essays and Conversations*, 158–78.) Excellent study of Doctorow's place in this subgenre.

Friedl, Herwig. "Power and Degradation: Patterns of Historical Process in the Novels of E. L. Doctorow" (in Friedl and Schultz, *A Democracy of Perception*, 19–44). Argues for the alteration of energy and entropy in Doctorow's vision.

Girgus, Sam. "A True Radical History: E. L. Doctorow." *The New Covenant: Jewish Writers and the American Idea.* Chapel Hill: University of North Carolina Press, 1984; 160–83. Best discussion of Doctorow as "Jewish novelist."

————. "In His Own Voice: E. L. Doctorow's *The Book of Daniel*" (in Friedl and Schultz, *A Democracy of Perception*, 75–90). Useful study of *Daniel*.

Gross, David. "Tales of Obscene Power: Money and Culture, Modernism and History in the Fiction of E. L. Doctorow." *Genre*, no. 13 (1980):71–92. (Reprinted in Trenner, *Essays and Conversations*, 120–50.) An extreme but useful examination of Doctorow's use of modernist formal devices as distancing strategies.

Harpham, Geoffrey Galt. "E. L. Doctorow and the Technology of Narrative."

PLMA 100, no. 1 (1985):81–95. The most perceptive and valuable examination of Doctorow's uses of narrative and of the primacy of narration to his vision.

Johnson, Diane. "The Righteous Artist: E. L. Doctorow." In *Terrorists & Novelists*, edited by Diane Johnson, pp. 141–49. New York: Knopf, 1982. A witty and insightful analysis of Doctorow's technical virtuosity and skill despite his predictable political preoccupations.

LeClair, Tom, and Larry McCaffery. "A Spirit of Transgression," *Anything Can Happen: Interviews with Contemporary American Novelists*. Urbana: University of Illinois Press, 1983. (Reprinted in Trenner, *Essays and Conversations*, 31–47.) Useful interview.

Levine, Paul. "The Writer as Independent Witness." Interview, March 1978, Canadian Broadcasting Corp. (Reprinted in Trenner, *Essays and Conversations*, 57–69.) Useful interview.

———. "A Multiplicity of Witness: E. L. Doctorow at Heidelberg." Symposium with Doctorow and students, Heidelberg 19 June 1985. Printed in Friedl and Schulz, *A Democracy of Perceptions*, 61–73. Interesting symposium in which Doctorow responds to German audience.

Lorsch, S. E. "*The Book of Daniel* as *Künstlerroman*: The Politics of Art." *Papers in Language and Literature* 18 (1982):384–97. Argues for the peculiar nexus of art and politics in *Daniel*.

Lubarsky, Jared. "History and the Forms of Fiction: An Interview with E. L. Doctorow." *Eiso Seinen* [Tokyo] 124 (1978):150–52. Interesting interview focusing on narrative techniques.

Nadel, Alan. "Hero and Other in Doctorow's *Loon Lake*." *College Literature* 14, no. 2 (1987):136–45. Interesting discussion of self-generating nature of protagonist in *Loon Lake* and Doctorow's debt to Nabokov.

Navasky, Victor. "E. L. Doctorow: 'I Saw a Sign.'" *New York Times Book Review* 28 September 1980, 44–45. Informative interview on the occasion of the publication of *Loon Lake*.

Plimpton, George. "The Art of Fiction." Interview with E. L. Doctorow. *Paris Review* 101 (1986):22–47. Revealing interview.

Saltzman, Arthur. "The Stylistic Energy of E. L. Doctorow." In Trenner, *Essays and Conversations*, 73–108. One of the few extended studies of the texture of Doctorow's work; valuable.

Schulz, Dieter. "E. L. Doctorow's America: An Introduction to His Fiction" (in Friedl and Schulz, *A Democracy of Perception*, 9–18). Excellent short introduction; German perspective.

Tanner, Stephen L. "Rage and Order in Doctorow's *Welcome to Hard Times*." *South Dakota Review* 22, no. 3 (1984):79–85. A wrong-headed but interesting study of the novel in the context of the traditional western.

Trenner, Richard. "Politics and the Mode of Fiction." *Ontario Review*, no. 16

(Spring–Summer 1982):5–16. (Reprinted in Trenner, *Essays and Conversations*, 48–56.) Useful interview.

Weber, Bruce. "The Myth Maker: The Creative Mind of Novelist E. L. Doctorow." *New York Times Magazine* 21 October 1985, 25–31. Good general assessment of Doctorow on the occasion of the publication of *World's Fair.*

Index

Abstract, 96
Accidental Tourist, The (Tyler, Anne), 105
Adirondack Mountain Region, 74, 89
Aesthetic, 38, 44, 49, 86, 95, 101
Africa, 2; *see* Hemingway, Ernest
Alger, Horatio, 81, 82
All the King's Men (Warren, Robert Penn), 81
Allegorical, 60
Alter, Robert, 5, 44
American Book Award, 3, 120
American Communists, 37
American consciousness, 43
American Dream myth, 81–84, 92
American Dream, An (Mailer, Norman), 81
American Gothic, 43
American history, 60
American idealism, 31
American novelists, 58
American Tragedy, An (Dreiser, Theodore), 81
American traitors, 31
American West, 18–20, 22
American western, 26
Anaheim, 44
Anarchistic, 37, 47
Anti-Emersonian (idealism), 31
Antihistorical, 59
Antirealistic, 59, 96
Archduke Franz Ferdinand, 51, 53, 65
Archer, Isabel (*Portrait of a Lady, The*), 73
Archetypal, 100
Archetypal nature of characterization, 57
Archetypal traitors, 31
Arctic, 50, 51, 65, 71
Armistice Day parade, 70
Arnold, Marilyn, 19
Arnold, Matthew, 12
Ashkenazy, Baron, 52, 66
Atlantic City, 52, 53
Autobiographical, 99, 107, 111
Autobiographical novel, 95

Autobiography, 106, 110, 118

Bar mitzvah, 45
Barnes, Jake (*Sun Also Rises, The*), 73
Barth, John, 7, 12, 13, 31, 35–36
Baudelaire, Charles, 21, 61
Bell, Pearl, 5, 72, 85
Bellow, Saul, 101
Belsen, 44
Biblical imagination, 29
Biblical namesake, Daniel, 32
Big as Life. See Doctorow, E. L.
Bildungsroman, 57, 72, 73; *see* Bronx bildungsroman
Billy Bathgate. See Doctorow, E. L.
Book of Daniel, The. See Doctorow, E. L.
Book-of-the-Month Club, 3
Brienza, Susan, 66
Bronx, 107, 113–15, 118
Bronx bildungsroman, 108
Bronx High School of Science, 2
Brown, Norman O., 92
Brownjohn, Alan, 79
Buchenwald, 44
Buck, Frank, 111
Buddha, 86
Buddhism, 86

California, 42, 45, 53, 74, 76–77, 82
Camus, Albert, 10
Capitalism, 47
Catharsis, 42
CBS Television, 3
CIA, 80, 83, 85, 104, 105
Central Park West, 101
Chance (Conrad, Joseph), 86
Charyn, Jerome, 39
Chase, Richard, 62
Cheever, John, 3
Cinematic nature of narrative line, 57
Circularity, 53, 65, 68
Claremont Park, 108

Clayton, John, 115
Colorado, 74
Columbia Pictures, 3
Columbia University, 2, 3, 26
Communism, 47
Communist, 26, 34
Communist Party, 40
Compson, Quentin (*Sound and the Fury, The*), 73
Concentric circles, 113, 116
Coney Island, 53
Connecticut, 100
Conrad, Joseph, as Polish expatriot, 85; "The Secret Sharer," 85; "Youth," 86; *see also Heart of Darkness*
Contingency, 26, 48, 71, 98
Contrapuntal, 14
Cooke, Michael G., 6
Cooper, Barbara, 11
Coover, Robert, 5, 7, 58, 59; *Public Burning, The,* 28
Cosmic reality, 9
Curran, Ronald, 79
Cyclical images, 70
Cynical, 22

Dakota apartments, New York City, 101
Darwin, Charles, 103
Dawson, Anthony, 65
Detroit, 33
Dial Press, 3, 24
Didion, Joan, 13
Dillard, Annie, 38
Disneyland, 29, 42–44, 117
Disynchrous, 86, 88
Doctorow, David and Rose (Parents), 2
Doctorow, E. L., background, 2–12; as film editor, 3, 13

WORKS-NOVELS:
Big as Life, 1, 3, 10, *23–26,* 57
Billy Bathgate, 120
Book of Daniel, The, 1, 3, 5, 7, 10–12, 25–26, 30, 34, 47, 49, 56, 57, 60, 62, 66, 70, 80, 84, 86, 106–107, 112, 117, 120

Drinks before Dinner, 1, 3, 31, 48, 95–100, 107
Lives of the Poets, 1–3, 94–95, 97, 99–107, 113–14, 118
Loon Lake, 1, 3, 5–7, 13, 66, 69, 72–73, 78–87, 90–93, 95, 99–100, 106, 112, 118, 120
Ragtime, 1, 3, 5, 7–9, 12–13, 49–50, 56–59, 61–63, 65–66, 68, 70–72, 79, 82, 86, 94, 97, 106, 112–13, 115, 118, 120
Welcome to Hard Times, 1, 3, 7, 10, 13–14, 18–19, 23–24, 26, 46–47, 49, 57, 66, 69, 71, 88, 99, 106, 120
World's Fair, 1, 3, 6–7, 67, 94, 99, 101, 106–108, 110–13, 116–17, 120

WORKS-PROSE:
"False Documents," 8, 21–22

Dos Passos, John, 8; *see U.S.A.*
Dostoyevski, Fyodor, 36
Dreiser, Theodore, 68
Drinks before Dinner. See Doctorow, E. L.
Dualism, 84
Dualistic persona, 80

Egypt, 52
El Salvador, 106
Electricity, 45
Electricity, as a topic and motif, 41
Elegiac, 20
Eliot, T. S., 8, 21; "Gerontion," 8; "Love Song of J. Alfred Prufrock, The," 28
Emblidge, David, 11
Emerald Isle Fire Station, 51–52
Emerson, Ralph Waldo, 4
Emersonian Idealism, 10
Encyclopedic design, 55
England, 53
Enlightenment, 19
Entropy, 11
Epistemological, 11, 23, 39, 86
Epstein, Joseph, 5
Estrin, Barbara L., 31, 47
Europe, 52, 67, 103, 115

European civilization, 70
European fascism, 113
European fiction, 58
European totalitarianism, 10
Evans, Thomas, 64
Existential, 11, 14, 31, 32, 38, 61, 81, 84
Existentialism, 10

Fascist, 44
Fatalistic, 19, 22
Faulkner, William, 13, 59
FBI, 28, 36, 37, 42
Feingold, Michael, 99
Feminist movement, 54
Fictionalizing history, 58
Film editor. *See* Doctorow, E. L.
Finn, Huck (*Adventures of Huckleberry Finn, The*), 73
Fitzgerald, F. Scott, 13; "Diamond as Big as the Ritz," 81
Flower, Dean, 79
Flushing Meadow, 117
Foley, Barbara, 8, 9
Ford, Henry, 8, 51, 53, 59, 69, 70
Ford, Richard, 13
France, 116
Freud, Sigmund, 9, 53–54, 60
Friedl, Herwig, 11

Galicia, 103
Gardner, John, 13
Gatsby, Jay (*Great Gatsby, The*), 73
German U-boat, 53
Germans, 116
Germany, 2, 70
Girgus, Sam B., 12
Godwin, Gail, 13
Goldman, Emma, 50, 52, 54, 59
Goodbye, Columbus (Roth, Philip), 81
Gordimer, Nadine, 4
Gordon, Mary, 13
Grapes of Wrath, The (Steinbeck, John), 81
Grass, Günter, 4
Gravity's Rainbow (Pynchon, Thomas), 59
Great Depression, 116
Great Gatsby, The (Fitzgerald, F. Scott), 13, 81, 82

Green, Martin, 61
Greenland, 65
Greenwich Village, 100
Gross, David, 31, 46
Grumbach, Doris, 56

Harlem, 65
Harpham, Geoffrey Galt, 31, 47, 85–87, 94
Hawthorne, Nathaniel, 10, 60, 63
Heart of Darkness (Conrad, Joseph), 28, 86; *see* Conrad, Joseph
Hebrew, 115
Hemingway, Ernest, 2, 13
Historian, 20, 23–24
Historical authenticity, 118
Historical events, 71
Historical figures, 50, 55, 60
Historical personages fictionalized, 7
Historical realism, 63
Historical repetition, 47
History, 8, 10–12, 58, 64, 68, 71–72, 81, 82, 87, 91, 94, 107
History and myth, 18
History, oral, 111
Hitler, Adolphe, 115–17
Hoffman, Abbie, 37
Hollywood, 92
Holocaust, 44
Houdini, Harry, 50, 53–54, 59, 61, 64–68, 71
Human perception, 11
Humanist, 9
Husserl, Edmund, 10

Icarus, 91
Ideologues, 6
Illusionary progress, 11
Images, 11
Images, of history, 8, 59
Imitative fallacy, 80, 98
Indians, 89–90
International PEN, Forty-eighth Annual Congress, 4
Irish immigrants, 51
Ironic, 14, 16, 28, 63
Ironic fictionalization, 68

Ironic tone, 56
Ironical, 46
Ironically, 53
Irony, 17, 33, 37–39, 44, 56, 70, 80, 83,
    90, 92, 101, 104, 107, 117
Irving, John, 13
Isolate, Isolation, 84, 100–101, 104–105

Jacksontown, Indiana, 76–77, 82
Japan, 77, 86
Japanese, 83
Jesus, 14
Jew, 9, 38, 54, 67, 92
Jewish, 2, 44, 45, 100, 103, 114–15
Jewish culture, 2, 114; *see also* Doctorow,
    E. L.: background
Jewish Humanist, Radical, 6, 32, 92,
    115; *see also* Doctorow, E. L.:
    background
Jewish immigrant, 50; *see also* Doctorow,
    E. L.: background
Jewish Welfare Board, 114
Jews, 115
Johnson, Diane, 89, 91–92
Joplin, Scott, 55, 66
Joyce, James, "Araby," 110; "Joycean,"
    108; Joycean epiphany, 87
Jung, Karl, 53, 60

Kaddish, 45
Kafka, Franz, 60; "Hunger Artist," 67
Keats, John, 54
Kenyon College, 2
Kitsch myth, 44
Konwicki, Tadeusz, 4
Korean War, 36
Kramer, Hilton, 5, 63
Kramer, Hilton, "Political Romance," 62
Kriegel, Leonard, 68
Kundera, Milan, 4, 6
Kunstlerroman, 47

L'Amour, Louis, 59
Latvia, 66
Lawrence, Massachusetts, 51
Levine, Paul (*E. L. Doctorow*), 5, 11, 12,
    24, 26, 63, 85, 92, 94, 109

Linguistic device, 95
Linguistic structure, 102
Literary classics, 81
Literary tradition, American, 72
Literary zeitgeist, 95
Lives of the Poets. See Doctorow, E. L.
Lives of the Poets (Johnson, Samuel), 101
Loon Lake. See Doctorow, E. L.
Lord Jim (Conrad, Joseph), 86
Lorsch, Susan E., 47
Los Angeles, 43, 77
Lost in the Funhouse (Barth, John), 35
Lowell, Robert, 34
Ludlow mine disaster, 74
Lusitania, 53, 70

McCaffery, Larry, 38
Mailer, Norman, 4, 7, 9, 24, 34
Malamud, Bernard, 101
Manichaean, 112
Marcus, Greil, 62–63, 68–69
Mardi (Melville, Herman), 24
Marx, Karl, 47, 92
Marxism, 34
Masks, 99
Maupassant, Henri René Albert, de, 54
Melville, Herman, 10
Metafiction, 87
Mexican Revolution, 52
Mexico, 65
Michael Koblhaas (Kleist, Heinrich von),
    70
Michener, James, 59
Milton, John, 54
Mimesis, 67
Mindish, Linda, 31
Mirror of the Sea, The (Conrad, Joseph), 85
Misogynistic, 100
Moby Dick (Melville, Herman), 81
Modernism, 60
Modernist, 31
Modernist tradition, 26
Moral Fiction (Gardner, John), 54–55
Morgan, J. P., 8, 51–53, 58–59, 69–70, 82
Morgan, Pierpont, 63, 64
Morrison, Toni, 6, 13
Moses, Joseph, 60, 71

Murray, Albert, 62
Myth, 70
Mythic history, 57
Mythologize, 62
Mythopoeic imagination, 12

Nabokov, Vladimir, 61
Naming, 85
Narcissistic, 101
Narrative experimentation, 30
Narrative perspective, 26
Nashville (film), 62
National Book Critics Award, 3
Nazis, American, 115
Nesbit, Evelyn, 50, 54, 69
Netherlands, 116
New American Library, 3
New Left politics, 26
New Rochelle, 3, 41, 50, 52, 69
New World, 115
New York, 36–37, 51, 75, 113
New York City, 2, 18, 52, 74, 96, 107, 113
New York culturati, 100
New York literary scene, 101
New York Shakespeare Festival, 95
New York University, 3
New Yorkers, 107
Newark, 33
Nihilistic, 14, 18
Nixon, Richard, 59
Nobel Prize for Peace, 96
Notes from Underground (Dostoyevski,
    Fyodor), 35
Novel, genre of, 8

Oates, Joyce Carol, 13
Objective correlative, 73
Objective reality, 19, 20
Odysseus myth, 73
Oedipal, 103, 114
Oedipal metaphor, 84
Ohio, 2; *see* Doctorow, E. L.: background
Omni-Americans (Murray, Albert), 62
Omniscient narrator, 64
Omniscient perspective, 24
Ontological, 11, 23
Optimism, 17, 23

Oregon, 77
Ovid, 65

Pacific Ocean, 77
Pale Fire (Nabokov, Vladimir), 81
Palestine, 115
Paradoxical imagery, 89
Paternity, 85
Paterson (Williams, William Carlos), 81
Paterson, New Jersey, 74
Peary, Admiral, 50, 67
Pentagon, 28, 34, 40, 42
Pessimism, 46
Philosophical paradox, 96
Picaresque, 86
Picaro, 80, 85
Pierce, Constance, 66
Pioneers, The (Cooper, James Fenimore), 20
Plato, 7
Play It as It Lays (Didion, Joan), 97
Poe, Edgar Allan, 10, 31
Poland, 117
Polemical, 92
Political deconstruction, 47
Political novel, 47
Political novels, 6
Portrait of the Artist as a Young Man
    (Joyce, James), 112; *see also* Joyce,
    James
Postmodernism, 60, 66
Postmodernist, 12, 30, 35
Postmodernist relativism, 32
Pragmentism, 37
Prelude, The (Wordsworth, William),
    112–13
Prescott, Peter, 1
Princeton University, 3
Proletarian, 92
Prynne, Hester (*Scarlet Letter, The*), 73
Public Burning, The. See Coover, Robert
Puritan, Puritans, 4, 58
Pynchon, Thomas, 7
Pyrotechnics, 119

Quixotic, 45

Rabbi, 45

Ragtime. See Doctorow, E. L.
Random, 46
Randomness, 37
Ransom, John Crowe, 2
Reagan, Ronald, 4
Realism, 12
Realpolitik, 4
Repetition, 11, 53, 69–71, 76, 88, 97–98
Repetition, meaningless, 11
Rilke, Rainer Maria, 106
Roach, Hal: "Our Gang," 70
Robeson, Paul, 35
Rodgers, Bernard F., 71
Rodgers, Bernard F., Jr., 49
Roosevelt, Franklin Delano, 115
Roosevelt, Teddy, 53
Rosenberg case, 28–29, 39
Rosenberg case, historical, 30
Rosenberg, Julius and Ethel, 5, 28–30, 40
Roth, Philip, 4, 13, 67, 101
Rousseauesque, 19
Rubin, Jerry, 37
Russia, 40
Russian Jewish Immigrants, 2; *see*
    Doctorow, E. L.: background

Sacco, Nicola, 30, 113
Sag Harbor, 3
Sale, Roger, 60, 62–63
Saltzman, Arthur, 18, 46, 81
Sarah Lawrence College, 3
Sartre, Jean Paul, 10
Satan, 54
Satire, 56
Satiric irony, 57
Satirical, 64
Scholes, Robert, 59
Schulz, Dieter, 12
Science fiction, 57
Scopes, John Thomas, 30
Secret Agent, The (Conrad, Joseph), 85; *see
    also* Conrad, Joseph
Seder, 114
Self-aware, 110
Self-caricature, 100
Self-conscious narrator, 85
Self-ironical, 110

Self-parodying, 100
Self-reflexive, 85, 100, 101
Self-reflexivity, 12, 30, 66, 107
Setzer, Helen, 2
Sherman, James, 52
Shultz, George, 4
Silhouette, 64, 66–68
Simon & Schuster, 24
Skepticism, 39, 46
Social themes, 53
Social value, 9
Socialism, 47
Socialism, American, 7
Solitude, 94
Solitude, in American literary history, 4
Solzhenitsyn, Alexander, 4
Sotweed Factor, The (Barth, John), 59; *see
    also* Barth, John
Sound and the Fury, The (Faulkner,
    William), 13, 73; *see also* Faulkner,
    William
Soviet Union, 39
Spain, Carlists conspirators, 85
Spanish revolution, 115
Staccato effect, 55
Sternlicht's critique of progress, 47
Stevens, Wallace, 80
Stimson, Henry, 40
Styron, William, 7
Sun Also Rises, The (Hemingway, Ernest),
    13; *see also* Hemingway, Ernest
Sutherland, John, 111
Swastika, 115
Synchronicity, 72, 88
Synchronous experiences, 83
Syncopate, syncopated, 70, 71
Syncopated prose, 68

Taft, William Howard, 53, 63–64
Tanner, Stephen L., 18
Television, 58, 96; impact on readers, 38
Thaw, Harry K., 50, 70
Theatre of ideas, 96
Theatre of language, 96
Third Reich, 44
Thoreau, Henry David, 4, 91; *see also
    Walden Pond*

Todd, Richard, 68–69
Tolstoy, Leo, 54
Tomorrowland, Disneyland, 44–45
Towers, Robert, 72
Trenner, Richard (*E. L. Doctorow: Essays and Conversations*), 2–3, 6–8, 12–14, 18–19, 23, 25, 30–31, 46–47, 59, 81, 93, 99, 115
Trilling, Lionel, 5
Truman, Harry S., 40
Twentieth-century perspective, 38

U.S.A. (Dos Passos, John), 8, 72, 81, 85
Ulysses (Joyce, James), 73; *see also* Joyce, James
United States, 28, 33, 63, 69, 105; United States of America, 60, 77
United States Army, 2
University of California at Irvine, 3
Updike, John, 3, 13

Vanzetti, Bartolomeo, 30, 113
ventriloquism; 110–11
ventriloquist, 80–81, 99
Vidal, Gore, 7
Vietnam, 40
Violence, 70
Virginian, The (Wister, Owen), 20

Waiting for Godot (Beckett, Samuel), 98
Walden Pond (Thoreau, Henry David), 81, 91
Washington, 42
Washington, Booker T., 52
Welcome to Hard Times. See Doctorow, E. L.
Western fiction, 57
Western Myth, 14
"Which Side Are You On" (Traditional Union Song), 37
WASP, 60
WASP, non, 117
White House, 42
White, Stanford, 50
Whitman, Walt, 81
Wilson, Woodrow, 53
Wolcott, James, 100
Worcester State Hospital, 29
Wordsworth, William, 61, 112
World War I, 53, 55
World's Fair. See Doctorow, E. L.
Wright, James, 2

Yale School of Drama, 3

Zapata, Emiliano, 52
Zen garden, 83